G000138095

VICTORIa CROSS WINNERS OF THE KOREAN WAR

1950–1953

VICTORIA CROSS WINNERS OF THE KOREAN WAR

1950–1953

STEPHEN WYNN

Pen & Sword

MILITARY

AN IMPRINT OF PEN & SWORD BOOKS LTD.
YORKSHIRE – PHILADELPHIA

First published in Great Britain in 2021 by
PEN & SWORD MILITARY
An imprint of
Pen & Sword Books Ltd
Yorkshire - Philadelphia

Copyright © Stephen Wynn, 2021

ISBN 978 1 52671 331 5

The right of Stephen Wynn to be identified as Author of this work has been
asserted by him in accordance with the Copyright, Designs and Patents Act 1988.

A CIP catalogue record for this book is available from the British Library

All rights reserved. No part of this book may be reproduced or transmitted in any
form or by any means, electronic or mechanical including photocopying, recording
or by any information storage and retrieval system, without permission from the
Publisher in writing.

Typeset in Ehrhardt MT & 12/16
by SJmagic DESIGN SERVICES, India.
Printed and bound by CPI Group (UK) Ltd, Croydon, CR0 4YY

Pen & Sword Books Ltd incorporates the imprints of Pen & Sword Archaeology,
Atlas, Aviation, Battleground, Discovery, Family History, History, Maritime,
Military, Naval, Politics, Social History, Transport, True Crime, Claymore Press,
Frontline Books, Praetorian Press, Seaforth Publishing and White Owl

For a complete list of Pen & Sword titles please contact

PEN & SWORD BOOKS LTD
47 Church Street, Barnsley, South Yorkshire, S70 2AS, England
E-mail: enquiries@pen-and-sword.co.uk
Website: www.pen-and-sword.co.uk

Or

PEN & SWORD BOOKS
1950 Lawrence Rd, Havertown, PA 19083, USA
E-mail: Uspen-and-sword@casematepublishers.com
Website: www.penandswordbooks.com

Contents

Sources   vi

Introduction   vii

Chapter One   Build up to the war   1

Chapter Two   Countries involved in the war   4

Chapter Three   Private Bill Speakman, VC   9

Chapter Four   Lieutenant Philip Kenneth Edward Curtis, VC   27

Chapter Five   Lieutenant Colonel James Power Carne, VC, DSO   34

Chapter Six   Major Kenneth Muir, VC   44

Chapter Seven   Lieutenant Terence Edward Waters, GC   60

Chapter Eight   Fusilier Derek Godfrey Kinne, GC   69

Chapter Nine   Korean war through the eyes of the press   78

Chapter Ten   Korean war   92

Chapter Eleven   British & Commonwealth Regiments in the
                   Korean war   104

In Closing   110

Appendix   The viewpoint of a modern soldier in combat   112

About the Author   115

Index   117

Sources

www.in2013dollars.com
Wikipedia.
www.distance.to
www.quora.com
www.fsmith.com
www.kosb.co.uk
www.vconline.org.uk
www.distancefromto.net
www.gc-database.co.uk
www.northeastmedals.co.uk
www.timefortruth.co.uk
www.dbpedia.org
www.cranhamlhs.org.uk

Introduction

This book is, in the main, about four men: Lieutenant Colonel James Power Carne, DSO; Major Kenneth Muir; Lieutenant Philip Kenneth Edward Curtis, and Private William Speakman, who were soldiers in the British Army and were awarded the Victoria Cross for their actions during the Korean war, 25 June 1950 – 27 July 1953.

It will also look at the awarding of the George Cross to Lieutenant Terence Edward Waters and Fusilier Derek Godfrey Kinne. The George Cross holds an equivalent level of importance to the Victoria Cross, but is awarded to civilians and military personnel who displayed conspicuous bravery that was not carried out in the face of the enemy.

To fully tell their story I have to provide you with some background, not only about each of these six brave men, but first about how they came to be fighting in a war 5,500 miles away, in a country that many of them would not only never have heard of, but probably wouldn't know where to find it on a map.

To achieve this, I will begin by looking at a timeframe that covers the period from May 1945 to June 1950, during the build-up to the outbreak of the war, and how and why the war started, just five years after the end of the Second World War. I will also touch on the war itself, relevant to the actions that saw each of the men awarded their medals.

Despite the Second World War having come to an end in 1945, there were numerous military conflicts which took place in the following years, as the world went through a period of readjustment. Countries and territories that had previously been ruled and occupied by other nations, wanted their freedom and independence in this big new world. There were some countries in the post war era, more commonly referred to as the Cold War, who, for want of a better word, became enslaved. In particular those who became satellite states of the Soviet Union, and were often referred to as Eastern Bloc countries. These included Poland, East Germany, Czechoslovakia, Hungary, Romania, Bulgaria, Albania and Yugoslavia. This not only made the Soviet Union a more powerful entity, but also acted as a security blanket to protect Mother Russia from any potential threat from the West.

Chapter One

Build up to the war

After the end of the Second World War, the Allied powers decided that the control of Korea, which had been annexed by Japan in 1910, would be shared. The move was only ever intended to be short term, prior to a return to Korean independence. The Soviet Union would take control of the north of the country above the 38th parallel, while the rest of the nation, south of that line, would be controlled by American military authorities under the command of General Douglas MacArthur.

Taking into account this was only ever intended to be for the short term, it was quite alarming to some in the political arena when not only did the Soviet Union oversee what was already in place, it also backed a Stalinist regime under Kim Il-sung, created the North Korean People's Army, and then equipped it with Russian tanks and artillery. In the south of the country, the political situation was somewhat chaotic, as one might expect during such changes to a country's normal way of life. This eventually led to an American-backed administration under President Syngman Rhee, who was determined to see his nation once again reunited, if not through political means, then by force if necessary. Unlike the Soviet Union's stance in the north, however, America had trained a South Korean army to be no more than a lightly armed gendarmerie. There had been no influx of heavily armoured American battle tanks or state-of-the-art combat aircraft, just a very limited number of artillery pieces.

All that had really been achieved by the division of the country was an atmosphere of mistrust, uncertainty, and a belief by either side that a new united Korea should be based on their model. This simply raised the tension between the two halves of the country, until it came to a head on 25 June 1950, when the North Korean People's Army crossed over the 38th parallel and began an invasion of the South. This would not have taken place without the direct intervention and approval of Joseph Stalin.

In response to the North's unprovoked actions, the United Nations sent a mainly American force to assist South Korean forces.

Strangely enough, despite North Korea being under the control of the Soviet Union, it was Chinese forces who fought alongside the North Korean People's Army, and by July 1953 it was estimated that the combined number of Korean and Chinese forces involved in the conflict had reached 1,200,000 men, so determined were they to overrun the South. When it came to the United Nations, they had a number of countries they could call upon to send troops to the stricken region to prevent the North from achieving their aims. Besides the United States and Britain, other countries including Australia, Canada, Columbia, France, Holland, the Philippines, and Turkey, also sent troops. It was the United States who made the largest contribution of troops and equipment with Britain second. By spring 1951 Britain's contribution to the troop numbers of the United Nation's forces had reached 12,000, and by 1952, the combined number of United Nations and Republic of Korea forces had reached 932,000.

The United Nations estimated that by the end of the war the total number of Koreans, both civilian and military forces, who had been killed on both sides was in the region of some 3 million people, while Chinese losses were put at around 900,000. The economic effect on the country as a whole was staggering, and there had been massive social upheaval for large parts of the civilian population. What made the situation even worse was the fact that neither side had actually won the war. The 38th parallel still divided the country.

American losses were recorded as 33,651, with more than 100,000 wounded. More than 100,000 British service personnel served during the Korean war, of whom more than 1,000 were killed. 2,674 were wounded, 179 reported missing in action and just under 1,000 taken as PoWs.

Technically, North and South Korea have remained at war ever since, although in 1991 they signed a non-aggression pact. The difference in the fortunes of the two countries has become vast. Today South Korea is a developed nation which currently has the twelfth largest economy in the world. But that was not always the case. After the end of the war in

July 1953, a period of social and economic instability followed, which in 1960 led to the April Revolution that saw mass protests against the South Korean President, Syngman Rhee, that lasted for sixteen days and cost the lives of 142 civilians, who were shot dead by the police. This resulted in the downfall of the government and the resignation of President Rhee, who fled to the United States.

In 1961, there was a military coup d'etat which brought with it a period of economic and social stability, and by 1965 South Korea had developed in such a way that she was able to send a number of her well trained troops to assist South Vietnam during the Vietnam war, support which continued until the end of that war. During that same timeframe the South Korean authorities received $235,560,000 in financial aid and military procurement.

For North Korea, it was a different story altogether. Extensive bombing by the United States Air Force during the war had virtually destroyed the North's industry. Things became so bad that the North Korean President, Kim Il-Sung, had to ask the Soviet Union for economic and industrial assistance. The Soviet government agreed to Kim's request and began by cancelling or postponing all of North Korea's debt. On top of this the Soviets agreed to pay £1 billion in monetary aid, which to provide some idea of perspective would, in 1953, have been worth approximately £11,500,000, which at today's value would be somewhere in the region of £323,000,000. But this was not all in cash, it also included industrial equipment as well as consumer goods. Other member states of the Soviet Union also assisted with a combination of logistical support, technical aid and medical supplies. China also played her part in helping to transform North Korea's situation by cancelling their war debt, as well as promising cooperation over trade deals, and sent thousands of her troops to help rebuild North Korea's broken infrastructure. As if that wasn't enough China also handed over ¥800 million, which at today's value would be worth nearly £7 billion.

Chapter Two

Countries involved in the war

Although the Korean war was fundamentally a civil war between the Communist – led northern half of the country against a democratically led southern half, there was a much bigger picture to the events. In essence this was a fight between two politically held beliefs, the communism and socialism of the Soviet Union against that of Western capitalism and democracy.

The Russian led Soviet Union wanted to increase the number of Communist countries under her control, while America in particular wanted to prevent communism when and wherever she could, regardless of the fact that Korea and the United States are separated by the Pacific Ocean and a distance of some 6,410 miles.

In the case of Korea, here was a country that in essence had been a closed state, especially to European countries, until about October 1873, when Yi Ha-ung, King Gojong's father, retired as regent. There then followed a period of instability throughout Korea, with many government officials supporting the idea of opening the country up to trade agreements with foreign powers, including France, the United Kingdom and the United States, all of whom had expressed an interest.

Throughout the early to middle 1800s there had been a number of attempts by Western countries to directly trade with Korea, all of which had been rebuffed. As early as 1832, the *Lord Amherst*, a vessel of the British East India Company, appeared off the north-west coast of Korea looking to trade, but her attempts were turned down. In 1845 HMS *Samarang* surveyed the southern coastal regions of Jeolla province and Jeju Island, although made no attempt to trade with the Koreans.

The south-west province of Chungcheong was the next part of Korea to experience a foreign ship at anchor in its coastal waters when three French vessels arrived in June 1846. On this occasion there was no attempt to seek trade, but to convey a letter of protest in relation to the persecution of Catholics throughout Korea. Two Russian vessels sailed along the country's north-east coast in April 1854. In an unprovoked act of aggression they opened fire, killing and injuring a number of Korean civilians inland. The German explorer and adventurer Ernst Oppert, made two unsuccessful attempts to conduct trade with the Koreans in 1866, and in the same year the crew of an American vessel, the *General Sherman*, also made attempts to trade, which were turned down. The Americans responded by kidnapping a Korean official and taking him on board their ship before the crew opened fire on Korean officials and civilians on shore. They followed that up by coming ashore and ransacking the town, killing a number of Koreans in the process. In an attempt to leave, the *General Sherman* ran aground in the Taedong River; Korean forces set fire to her, killing all twenty-three members of her crew.

In 1875 Japan, who saw Korea as a weaker nation, recognised an opportunity to exert political and economic pressure on Korea for her own benefit, before another country managed to do so.

Japan's influence over Korea can be dated to what history has recorded as the 'Ganghwa incident', which took place on 20 September 1875 when fighting broke out between Korean land forces and the Japanese gunboat, the *Un'yo*. Korean defensive forts opened fire on the Japanese vessel from Ganghwa Island, which resulted in the *Un'yo* returning fire and disabling the Korean Forts. She attacked another Korean Fort on the nearby Yeongjong Island, before returning to Japan. On 26 February 1876 Korea signed the Ganghwa Treaty, which gave many more rights to Japan than it did to Korea.

Following the signing of the Japan-Korea Treaty on 22 August 1910, Korea was ruled and occupied by Japan; this resulted in Japan's annexation of Korea, which remained in place until the Japanese surrender at the end of the Second World War. It was at this point that Korea was divided in to the territories of North and South Korea.

Insofar as fighting troops on the ground, North Korea's only ally was China, but the Korean war cannot be spoken about without mentioning the Soviet Union and the part she played in it. It was Soviet troops, along with those from the United States of America, who liberated Korea from Japanese control at the end of the Second World war, and they remained above the 38th parallel until they left in 1948.

I have written elsewhere in this book that Kim Il-sung, the Communist leader of North Korea, sought permission from Stalin in March 1953 to invade South Korea, despite the fact that Soviet forces had left North Korea five years earlier. Stalin, who did not want a direct military confrontation with America, told Kim Il-sung that he needed to speak with China's Mao Zedong for his support in any land war – not something that China was going to say no to, as she badly needed and wanted the economic support and military hardware that the Soviet Union was prepared to supply her with. Stalin's direct support to the North Koreans was by way of arming them with weapons and ammunition.

As mentioned above, China was heavily involved in the Korean war. As early as the latter months of 1949, Mao sent two divisions of the People's Liberation Army, which consisted mainly of Korean-Chinese troops. This was further supplemented by more troops as the year drew to an end. These were not poorly armed new recruits, these were well trained, disciplined, and experienced soldiers, who were in possession of up-to-date weapons as well. With all of this support, North Korea was as prepared as she could possibly be.

The down side for North Korea was that she wasn't up against just the relatively inexperienced forces of South Korea, she was up against the numerous countries of the United Nations, which were many. The United States of America undoubtedly being the biggest and most powerful, although her credibility wasn't helped any when General William Lynn Roberts, the man in charge of the Korean Military Advisory Group, said that any North Korean invasion would merely provide target practice for South Korean forces. How wrong is it possible for one man to be?

Below is a complete list of the countries who under the auspices of United Nations, sent ground troops to take part in the Korean war:

South Korea
United States of America
United Kingdom
Canada
Turkey
Australia
Philippines
New Zealand
Thailand
Ethiopia
Greece
France
Columbia
Belgium
South Africa
Holland
Luxembourg

Next is a list of countries who provided medical support only:

Denmark
Italy
West Germany
India
Israel
Norway
Sweden

Finally, a list of nations who provided other types of support, such as medical supplies, food, water, and blankets:

Taiwan
Japan

Pakistan
Cuba
El Salvador
Spain

Some members of the United States government expressed concern about becoming involved in such a war. While some considered it was necessary in order to prevent the spread of worldwide communism, for others, the opposite was the case. For them the concern was that their presence in South Korea would automatically bring the Soviet Union in to the war. But maybe the real consideration for President Truman and his government was the uncertainty over North Korea's invasion of the south. Was it a Soviet attempt to drag the United States in to a war, or was it simply just a test of America's resolve, to see if she would waver in the face of adversity? While she was treading water on what course of action to take, the American government received word from Russia on 27 June 1950, that she would not intervene if the United States sent ground forces to South Korea.

There is a certain irony about this whole affair, because it appears that America only sent ground troops to Korea because the Soviet Union gave them the green light to do so, despite the fact that they were supplying the North Koreans with ammunition, weapons and other military hardware.

Chapter Three

Private Bill Speakman, VC

When I began researching material for this book, the first thing I did was to look up the names of those men about whom I would be writing. I soon discovered that only one of the four men concerned was still alive, Sergeant Bill Speakman. The awards to Lieutenant Philip Kenneth Edward Curtis, and Major Kenneth Muir were both given posthumously, and Colonel James Power Carne passed away on 19 April 1986, just eight days after his 80th birthday.

My starting point was to try and locate Bill Speakman, as I simply didn't have a clue where he lived. I wasn't even sure that he lived in the United Kingdom. I eventually found out that he was a resident at the Royal Hospital Chelsea. I contacted the hospital by e-mail in early November 2016, introduced myself, explained that I was going to be writing a book about the Victoria Crosses awarded during the Korean war and that if possible, I would like to interview Bill Speakman, who I understood was an in-patient at the Hospital.

I received a reply from the Captain of Invalids Number One Company informing me that Bill had agreed to be interviewed and after a few more emails, the date was set for the afternoon of 2 February 2017.

I duly arrived at the Royal Hospital Chelsea at the allotted time and date, and was met by Rupert, the Captain of Invalids Number One Company. After a brief conversation and some pleasantries I was shown in to a dining room where I waited for Bill to arrive. Not more than five minutes had gone by when I looked up and saw a guy in a wheelchair being pushed along a corridor towards us. When he arrived I instinctively stood up; I don't know why, it just seemed the right thing to do.

'Don't be daft man, sit yourself down,' he said quietly, and with the hint of a smile on his face. 'I like the tattoos,' he said glancing at my arms, which led on to a brief conversation about why, when and where they were done.

From my research on Bill, I knew he had been born in Altrincham, Cheshire, on 21 September 1927, and had attended the Wellington School in Timperley, in what is now Greater Manchester. He had joined the army in 1945, and so keen had he been to enlist and get involved in the action that he'd lied about his age, saying that he was 18, when in fact he was only 17½.

I also knew that he left the army in 1967 after twenty-two years of service, and at one stage he fell on hard times and had to resort to selling his Victoria Cross to pay for a new roof on the cottage he was living in at the time. He was later presented with a genuine replacement by the British authorities.

While serving in Korea, he was wounded in the shoulder and leg by shrapnel while fighting against Chinese forces on Hill 217 and ended up in hospital in Japan. Remarkably, after he had recovered from his wounds he didn't return to the United Kingdom, instead he went back to Korea, where he found himself in a transit camp. He hadn't been there that long when he was instructed to go and see the camp commandant. Smartly dressed in his uniform, he stood to attention in front of the officer and saluted. He was asked to confirm his name, rank and serial number, which he did. The conversation continued about the state of his wounds, to which Bill responded by saying that he was OK and simply wanted to return to his regiment and his comrades. It was then that the commandant calmly informed him that he had been awarded the Victoria Cross and handed him a medal ribbon of his award. When he eventually returned to his regiment, the ribbon was pinned on his chest by a senior officer in front of the other members of his battalion.

Before we began chatting in earnest about the book I was going to be writing, a tray of tea, coffee and biscuits was brought over to the table.

'Help yourself,' he said pointing to the refreshments.

As a general rule I don't tend to be intimidated that easily, but my first impression of Bill Speakman, who was then 89 years of age, was that I would not have wanted to get on the wrong side of him in his heyday. He had white hair and beard, but even sat back, looking relaxed in his wheelchair, he still had a look about him, one that is hard for me to define on these pages, but I am sure some of you reading this will understand what I mean.

'So,' I said before checking myself. 'My apologies, but without being presumptuous, is it OK to call you Bill?'

He smiled, 'Of course it is.'

'OK Bill, to start with tell me about your childhood and how you came to join the army?'

That was the start of four cups of coffee and nigh on a two-hour conversation that just flowed from start to finish, with details of Bill's twenty-two-year career in the military, and a number of anecdotes of Bill's more than colourful life. Some of which were relevant to this story, and many that were not, but they were still very interesting to hear about.

He told me the story of how he had enlisted in the army when he was 17 but had lied about his age and told the recruiting officer that he was actually 18, knowing full well that if he hadn't told a little white lie, he wouldn't have been allowed to enlist. He had set his heart on a life in the military and didn't want to wait around for a year before he could become a soldier. Before he had completed his basic training, however, the Second World War was over.

Bill didn't want to be stuck back at home in a barracks in some forgotten part of the country, he wanted to be soldiering, and so volunteered for overseas postings, which was how he eventually ended up serving in Korea.

In the early part of 1951, Bill and his comrades from the 1st Battalion, King's Own Scottish Borderers were in Palestine, involved with internal security. After that they were in Hong Kong, and it was from there that they were sent to Korea, arriving at Inchon on 23 April 1951, where they were almost immediately sent in to action, with very little in the way of time to acclimatise to their new environment. The regiment's resources had become somewhat stretched after the end of the Second World War; the 6th and 7th Battalions were disbanded in 1946, and the 2nd Battalion suffered the same fate in 1947.

I eventually got round to asking Bill the question, 'If you will, tell me exactly what you did to win the Victoria Cross?'

It was a question Bill seemed somewhat uncomfortable with, not in hearing, but answering. I almost had to drag a reply out of him.

'I was just doing my job. They were trying to kill me and my friends, and I for one didn't want to die, and remember, it wasn't just me. There were others who did just as much as I did. It wasn't just me who was there fighting, it was an entire battalion of men, none of whom wanted to die or be captured and become a prisoner of war, so we all fought as hard as we could. It wasn't about being brave or courageous, we just did what we had been trained to do, and what we had to do that night to survive.'

I knew he was being modest with his answer, trying to play down his part in the events of that night in Korea, which then made it slightly awkward for me. The last thing I wanted was to appear rude or disrespectful, but I knew there was a lot more involved in what he had done, if for no other reason than I knew that no one was awarded the Victoria Cross simply for just 'doing their job'.

I unzipped my bag and took out *Two Sons in a Warzone – Afghanistan. The True Story of a Fathers Conflict*, a book I had written about my sons. I laid it on the table in front of Bill.

'I wrote this book, it was about my two sons. One of them was injured and the other was shot during their first tours of Afghanistan in 2009. They knew I was writing the book and were OK with it, but they both told me not to try and make them out to be heroes, because that's not how they saw themselves. For both of them, the heroes were their comrades who did not make it back.'

Bill didn't say a word, he didn't shake or nod his head, he just sat and looked at the book in front of him.

I was very conscious that not only were these events which had taken place some sixty-five years previously, but they had also required him to kill other human beings, albeit enemy soldiers who were trying to kill him at the time. But he didn't just kill one or two, a conservative estimate would put the number in the hundreds. His actions that night might well have left him with inner demons which he had to deal with, so the last thing I wanted to do was to open up a 'wound' that he had dealt with mentally many years before.

'What I am saying here Bill, is that although I understand your modesty about what you did to be awarded the Victoria Cross, we both know you did a great deal more than just doing your job. I don't want to make you feel uncomfortable about this, that's not what I want to do at all, but I do want to get it right, so that people know what it was you and your comrades did back in November 1951.'

He didn't say anything at first, but then he nodded and looked up. 'We were in a defensive position on what was known as Hill 217,' he said, 'and we had been there for a couple of weeks if I remember correctly. There had been a few little incidents during that time where they had a go at us, but nothing too serious, it was like they were testing us out, seeing what we were made of. What it did do was give us time to reinforce our positions just in case there was an all-out attack. We placed barbed wire in front of where we were, and had extra ammunition, grenades, food and water brought up.

'The fact they were having a go at us was somewhat strange as there were peace talks going on at the time in Panmunjom, Korea, which included representatives of the Korean People's Army, the Chinese People's Volunteer Army and the United Nations.'

Bill paused momentarily to take a sip of his drink before continuing.

'I was just a soldier, a private in the army doing my job to the best of my ability, as was everybody else. We had a job to do and that was it, really. We did what we were trained to do. Fight, hold our positions, and do whatever it took to stay alive.'

Knowing there was more detail to what had happened, I had to push him a little bit more, but I didn't want to irritate him and risk him stopping the interview; after all, he was doing me the favour by agreeing to meet me.

'It was only afterwards that I was told there were thousands of them charging up the hill trying to knock us off it,' he continued, 'and it didn't take a genius to work out that we were never going to be able to account for all of them with just bolt-action rifles, some of which didn't even work because it was so bloody cold.'

It was like reading a book and not being able to wait to turn the next page over to find out what happened next.

'So what did you decide to do next?'

'It was really cold, and I mean cold, so cold in fact that the ground was rock hard. I had worked out that the grenades wouldn't stick when they hit the ground, but bounce, so I grabbed hold of a couple of my guys, and we picked up as many grenades as we possibly could. As the Chinese started making their way up the hill towards us we started throwing the grenades at them and they bounced their way down the hill, scattering the enemy troops before detonating among them. This also gave us a bit of a breather as those who were not injured or killed had to dive to the ground to avoid the blast, which greatly slowed down their attack, and gave us the opportunity to throw more grenades at these guys who wanted to kill us.'

'And how long did all of this go on for?' I enquired. Bill sat back in his chair, and glanced up at the ceiling.

'I think it was for about six or seven hours, something like that, anyway.'

I couldn't help thinking that those six or seven hours, besides possibly being the longest six or seven hours of his life, also changed his life for ever.

The positions which the 1st Battalion, King's Own Scottish Borderers were holding, had previously been held by Chinese forces, but had been attacked and taken by five divisions of United Nations forces the previous month. The position covered a width of about 3,000 metres, making it very manpower intensive to defend.

The tactic deployed by the Chinese was very similar to that of the British and Allied forces before their infantry made their way across no man's land during the Somme Offensive in July 1916. Bombard the enemy's defensive position with artillery for a period of time and once finished, attack on foot. The Chinese didn't just attack the defensive line being held by the King's Own Scottish Borderers, they also aimed at positions behind the front lines, such as supply routes, using shells which exploded in the air, sending shards of shrapnel downwards, obliterating anything in its path.

The bombardment by the Chinese had begun at around noon on 4 November 1951, and at 4pm the same day, not only was it still going on, but had increased in its intensity. This was a sign for Bill and his comrades to make sure they were paying attention. The Chinese forces attacked soon after, but the artillery bombardment didn't stop – even when their 6,000 men reached the lines of the King's Own Scottish Borderers.

I had to politely laugh with an element of disbelief as Bill explained that when he was informed he had been awarded the Victoria Cross, he didn't even know what it was, or why the guys alongside whom he had been fighting hadn't been awarded the same medal.

Bill later became a member of the Special Air Service, which saw him serving in Malaya during what was known by the British as the Malayan Emergency – a guerrilla war that continued for twelve years between 1948 and 1960. The fighting was between Commonwealth forces and the pro-independence fighters of the Malayan National Liberation Army, which was the military wing of the Malayan Communist Party. At the time, Malaya was part of the British Empire and the fighting was over attempts by the Malayan Communist forces to gain independence and set up a socialist society. The old adage of there being two sides to every story, was true in this case, because what the British colonial authorities referred to as the 'Malayan Emergency' or 'The Emergency', the Malayan National Liberation Army, referred to as the 'Anti-British National Liberation War'.

What had always struck me as being strange was how fighting, which continued over a period of twelve years, could be referred to by the British authorities as an 'emergency', the definition of which is 'imminent'. I subsequently found out that it was called an 'emergency' purely for insurance purposes, because if it had been classed as a war, or specifically a civil war, British companies in Malaya affected by the fighting would not have been paid compensation by their London-based insurers for losses and damage they had incurred.

I asked Bill what he remembered from his time in the jungles of Malaya, and while he contemplated his reply, a smile appeared on his face.

'Funnily enough what I remember most about my time in the jungles of Malaya, is Singapore.'

At first I was slightly confused by his answer, but when he elaborated, it all became much clearer.

'When we came out of the jungle after having been in there for about three months or so, we would go to Singapore for some well-deserved R and R [rest and recreation].'

'I assume that required you to drink the odd beer or two?' I jokingly enquired. Bill laughed.

'Yes, I did drink a few beers that's for sure, it was just how we let our hair down after having been stuck in a jungle for a few months.'

'So how did you cope with the change of life in the jungle to the lights and glitter of the Singapore night-life?'

'Let's just say that we enjoyed ourselves with a few beers most nights, but the MPs (Military Policemen) could be buggers.'

'How's that?' I asked.

'They would always pick on me and my mates, and that didn't normally end well. I lost my sergeant's stripes on more than one occasion for fighting with the MPs.'

'Why did they pick on you? Surely you must have been doing something to have attracted their attention?'

'Most of the time it was because of my Victoria Cross, but it was also because they knew that me and my mates were members of the Special Air Service. It made them feel big, or good about themselves, if they could arrest me and then brag about having nicked a bloke who had won the Victoria Cross and was also a member of the Special Air Service. That's just how it was. They would turn up at the particular bar we were drinking at, words would be exchanged, they would then try and arrest a few of us, and then a fight would start. All we wanted to do was relax with a few drinks and let our hair down before it was time for us once again to return to the jungle. It just seemed to me that on some occasions, certain members of the Military Police were just spoiling for a fight, or some kind of confrontation with us.'

Bill Speakman was also involved in the Radfan Campaign that took place between January and May 1964, which was a series of military actions undertaken by elements of the British Army, during the Aden Emergency. Their opponents were the Front for the Liberation of

Occupied South Yemen, an Arab Nationalist military organisation, and the Marist paramilitary organisation, the National Liberation Front.

To provide the reader with some kind of understanding of just how ferocious the fighting was, on 29 April 1964, when a patrol led by Captain Edwards was attacked, he, along with Sapper John Warburton, was captured, taken prisoner and then killed. They were both decapitated and their heads displayed in the Yemeni capital. An extremely barbaric act, even in a war-type situation.

After I had finished interviewing Bill, he asked if I would like to come back to his room so I could look at his medals and take a few photographs. Bill's room was like something you would find in a five star hotel. There were a number of photographs of him from his days in the army and others of him looking resplendent in his Chelsea Pensioner's uniform. I noticed the set of ten medals on the breast of his Chelsea uniform tunic, and was pleased to see that I had two of the same medals that he had (Queen Elizabeth II Golden Jubilee and Diamond Jubilee medals). I then turned to my right, and on the wall I saw the citation for the award of his Victoria Cross, and what it said was a bit more than, 'I was just doing my job.'

> The King has been graciously pleased to approve the award of The Victoria Cross to:
>
> 14471590 Private William Speakman,
> Black Watch (Royal Highland Regiment),
> Attached to the 1st Battalion, The King's Own Scottish Borderers,
> in recognition of gallant and distinguished services in
> Korea.

From 0400 hours 4th November 1951, the defensive positions held by 1st Battalion, The King's Own Scottish Borderers were continuously subjected to heavy and accurate enemy shell and mortar fire. At 1545 hours this fire became intense and continued thus for the next two hours, considerably damaging the defences and wounding a number of men.

At 1645 hours the enemy in their hundreds advanced in wave upon wave against the King's Own Scottish Borderers' positions and by 1745 hours fierce hand to hand fighting was taking place on every position.

Private Speakman, a member of B Company Headquarters, learning that the section holding the left shoulder of the company's position had been seriously depleted by casualties, had had its NCOs wounded and was being overrun decided on his own initiative to drive the enemy off the position and keep them off it. To effect this he collected quickly a large pile of grenades and a party of six men. Then displaying complete disregard for his own personal safety, he led his party in a series of charges against the enemy; and continued doing so as each successive wave of enemy reached the crest of the hill. The force and determination of his charges broke up each successive enemy onslaught and resulted in an ever mounting pile of enemy dead.

Having led some ten charges, through withering enemy machine gun and mortar fire, Private Speakman was eventually severely wounded in the leg. Undaunted by his wounds he continued to lead charge after charge against the enemy and it was only after a direct order from his superior officer that he agreed to pause for a first field dressing to be applied to his wounds. Having had his wounds bandaged, Private Speakman immediately rejoined his comrades and led them again and again forward in a series of grenade charges, up to the time of the withdrawal of his company at 2100 hours.

At the critical moment of the withdrawal, amid an inferno of enemy machine gun and mortar fire, as well as grenades, Private Speakman led a final charge to clear the crest of the hill and hold it, while the remainder of his company withdrew. Encouraging his gallant but by now sadly depleted party, he assailed the enemy with showers of grenades and kept them at bay sufficiently long for his company to effect its withdrawal.

Under the stress and strain of this battle, Private Speakman's outstanding powers of leadership were revealed and he so dominated the situation that he inspired his comrades to stand firm and fight the enemy to a standstill. His great gallantry and utter contempt for his own personal safety were an inspiration to all his comrades. He was, by his heroic actions, personally responsible for causing enormous losses to the enemy, assisting his company to maintain their position for some hours and saving the lives of many of his comrades when they were forced to withdraw from their position.

Private Speakman's heroism under intense fire throughout the operation and when painfully wounded was beyond praise and is deserving of supreme recognition.

Extract from the *London Gazette* 28 December 1951.

A unique fact about Bill Speakman's Victoria Cross, was that although it was King George Vl who approved its award, it was actually his daughter, Queen Elizabeth ll, who presented it to him. King George Vl died on 6 February 1952, and Bill Speakman was presented with his Victoria Cross at Buckingham Palace in what was the first Victoria Cross that Her Majesty invested.

When my time with Bill came to an end, I was seen out by the guy who had helped him to the dining room where I had interviewed him. He was a friend of Bill's and a fellow in-pensioner at the hospital by the name of Paul Whittick; he had served in the army with the Royal Army Medical Corps.

'You're honoured,' he said with a smile.

'Sorry, what do you mean?' I said, not sure what he was talking about.

'Bill has done a few similar interviews with people over the years, and if he doesn't like them or is getting bored and fed up, he normally winds it up after about half-an-hour, but you have been with him for well over two hours.'

Paul's comments were certainly nice to hear and I had enjoyed my time with Bill. He certainly was a character, that's for sure, and came across as a kind and caring individual. As I was leaving his room he even said to us, 'you and I are friends for life now. If there's ever anything I can do for you, just let me know. Next time you are in London, if you are looking for somewhere to stay, I can get you in here, and you are always welcome to pop in and eat here anytime.'

The Royal Hospital at Chelsea and its grounds are certainly a grand setting, and a better location for an ageing soldier would be hard to find anywhere in the world.

In a ceremony which took place in the South Korean capital of Seoul on 21 April 2015, for visiting veterans of the Korean war, Bill Speakman presented a replica of his Victoria Cross along with the other medals he had been awarded, to the people and government of South Korea. A moving gesture that was appreciated by the nation's people.

The Liverpool Echo of Saturday 29 December 1951, included the following article about Private Bill Speakman.

Korean VC Nearly Forgot His Ribbon
'Lot did what I did.'

The second Victoria Cross ribbon to come to Korea arrived today wrapped in an old handkerchief in the pocket of Private William Speakman, hero of last month's 'Charlie Chinaman Gunpowder Plot' battle.

Major General A.J. Cassels, commander of the Commonwealth Division, will pin the ribbon on the 24-year-old Cheshire man's chest at a special parade tomorrow.

For nearly an hour after he arrived in Korea by air from Japan, where he has been in hospital since the battle, the shy burly soldier forgot all about the ribbon they had given him in Japan to bring with him.

In conversation with his company second in command, Captain R.H. Oates, who fought alongside Speakman and the rest of his King's Own Scottish Borderers company in the battle, he suddenly remembered it.

'I nearly forgot to give you this sir,' he said, carefully taking his handkerchief from a tunic pocket, removing the purple ribbon and handing it over.

'They said in Japan there might not be one over here.'

Captain Oates said he would pass the ribbon on to General Cassels.

In the Commonwealth Division's corporals' mess, Private Speakman read for the first time a copy of the citation for the award.

When he finished, he looked up and said, 'You know, I did not really lead anybody. There were a lot of chaps who did what I did.'

Reuters correspondent, Michael Ramsden, who flew with Private Speakman from Japan, said that the modest young soldier answered questions politely but a little reluctantly, as though he did not like talking about himself.

When the courier plane flew through bumpy weather over the Sea of Japan, his answers became briefer and briefer as it grew rougher. He was airsick. 'Give me good old terra firma every time,' he said, as the plane came down to land.

Speakman, a taciturn giant, managed to tuck his great bulk in to a buckled seat so unobtrusively, he was scarcely noticed by his fellow passengers

He said that beer played an important role in the 'gunpowder plot' battle. They had not had time to use the beer ration before the fighting started.

'I saw mortar crews cooling the barrels of their mortars with beer. When we ran out of grenades, we threw beer bottles and stones. I can remember very little about the battle now. We were at it so hard that I did not have time to notice the details,' he said in his very quiet voice.

He described how the action became just a blur of confused fighting. He did not realise how long it had gone on for before the order came to withdraw.

Speakman is unmarried. His twice widowed mother, Mrs Hanna Houghton, lives at 27 Moss Lane, Altrincham. He has been in the army for seven years, joining when he was 17, and went to Korea last June.

The first he knew of his Victoria Cross was when a senior officer broke the news to him in Kure, where he was waiting for transport from hospital back to his battalion in Korea.

Speakman said he had not considered the privileges which go with the Victoria Cross, which by custom include salutes from officers. He got his first salute from Australian Wing Commander, Keith Hennock, who wished him farewell from Iwakuni airfield.

Giving his account of the battle, Private Speakman said it was 'quite a little scrap. We had boxes of grenades pilled in a ration tent behind us. There was Sergeant Duncan, Corporal Wood, Corporal Wilson, Private Paddy Buchanan, and our Sergeant Major, Busty Murdoch. We kept making trips up to the crest of the hill and tossing grenades at the Chinese as they came.'

When mortar bomb shrapnel hit him in the leg for the first time, 'it felt just as if a stone had hit me'. Someone ordered him to the first aid station to get his wounds dressed. 'I got down there and there were a lot of badly wounded men, so I put a field dressing on my wound. It was not much at all.'

A medical orderly was hit in the back by shrapnel when he went out of the dugout to bring in a wounded man.

'I came back mad. Anyone would have felt mad at a thing like that,' he said.

He had 'a few more dabbles' at the Chinese after that.

The bit in the article about his medal ribbon and the medical orderly who was hit in the back by shrapnel were not things he told me about when I interviewed him at the Royal Hospital, Chelsea, but he did massively play down his part in what had happened. On more than one occasion he took our conversation on to other topics, and on each occasion I had to politely bring him back to telling me about his life and the events leading up to him being awarded the Victoria Cross. I can concur wholeheartedly with the Reuters correspondent who wrote the above article, when he says that Bill Speakman did not feel totally comfortable talking about what he did. He certainly did try and play it down.

Another article about Bill Speakman appeared the same day in the *Northern Whig* newspaper under the heading:

Black Watch Private Wins VC in Korea

Private William Speakman, of the Black Watch, seeing a British company hard pressed and hammered by shell and mortar fire in a day long battle on the Korean front on November 4, collected a few men and piles of grenades and led many charges. He fought the enemy to a standstill.

Even though wounded, he continued to cover the withdrawal of the company, dominating the position, and causing enormous losses to the enemy as they advanced in waves to the crest of the hill. His heroism has been rewarded with the Victoria Cross, the second of the Korean war, announced in last nights 'London Gazette'.

Private Speakman was attached to the 1st Battalion, King's Own Scottish Borderers.

Aged 24, on September 21, he enlisted as a regular on August 10, 1945.

The first Victoria Cross of the Korean war was won by Major Kenneth Muir, of The Argyll and Sutherland Highlanders, who was mortally wounded on September 23, 1950. The posthumous award was announced on January 5. Major Muir died leading remnants of two companies in an assault on Hill 282 in South Korea and was hit while firing mortar shells at advancing waves of enemy troops.

The announcement of the award to Private Speakman was made on the 47th birthday of his widowed mother, Mrs Hannah Houghton, who lives in a four roomed cottage at Altrincham. It came in the form of a telegram of congratulations from 'past and present pals' of the Black Watch Regiment at Perth.

Mrs Houghton said; 'I was sitting by the fire having five minutes rest when the telegraph boy arrived. What a wonderful birthday present it was. He is a very thoughtful boy. He sends 10s 6d home each week to pay for the rent. You can imagine I'm right proud of Bill, but then I knew he would do well in the army. He would have never settled down at work because he was so keen to join.'

Private Speakman will leave a British base hospital at Kure in Japan today and fly to Korea to receive the ribbon of the Victoria Cross from British Commander, Major General Jim Cassels.

Speakman said, 'I should like to write to my mother, as she will no doubt want to hear all about this.'

What a lovely surprise for Bill's mother, especially on her birthday. Bill's father had served in the First World War as a sergeant in the Black Watch and had died in 1948 from his wounds.

After Bill had recovered from his injuries, it was initially unclear whether he would return to his unit in Korea or be sent back home to England. His thoughts on the matter were:

> I should like to be going home, I suppose. But it is good to be back with the boys. The King's Own Scottish Borderers are a grand bunch of chaps.

Sadly, Bill Speakman passed away on 20 June 2018 at the Royal Hospital Chelsea at the age of 90; on 19 February 2019, in line with his dying wish, he was buried in the United Nations Memorial Cemetery in South Korea.

Bill Speakman's Victoria Cross is on display at the National War Museum of Scotland, in Edinburgh Castle, allowing visitors to read about the brave and heroic actions of an adopted son, that was William 'Bill' Speakman.

Casualties

On the night of 4/5 November 1951, the battalion was holding a position on a narrow ridge that was situated in the Kowang-San region of Korea. During the course of 4 November, the men of the King's Own Scottish Borderers were subjected to a concentrated and determined artillery and mortar bombardment. With nightfall the Chinese sent a division of their troops, numbering some 6,000 men. Although the companies' forward positions were overrun, the battalion as a whole held its ground, repulsing the sustained Chinese attack. By the break of dawn on 5 November 1951, twenty-eight officers and men of the battalion had been killed, with ninety having been wounded, and a further twenty being captured and taken as prisoners of war.

These are the names of those who were killed:

Apter, Private L.G., killed in action on 4 November 1951
Brady, Private H.M., killed in action on 5 November 1951
Collins, Private F., killed in action on 4 November 1951*
Crellin, Private R., killed in action on 4 November 1951
Dowie, Private T.M., killed in action on 4 November 1951
Edmund, Private W.A.M., killed in action on 4 November 1951
Foster, Private D.M., killed in action on 4 November 1951
Haldane, Private T., killed in action on 4 November 1951
Hobbs, Private A.E., killed in action on 4 November 1951
Kerr, Corporal Kerr, J.F., killed in action on 4 November 1951
Lockett, Private E., killed in action on 5 November 1951
McHale, Private C., killed in action on 4 November 1951*
McKeile, Private D., killed in action on 4 November 1951
McKendrick, Private R., killed in action on 4 November 1951
McLachlan, Private J.C.L., killed in action on 4 November 1951
McMillan-Scott, Lieutenant A.H.F., killed in action on 4 November 1951
Mackin, Private J., killed in action on 5 November 1951
Morris, WO2 J., killed in action on 4 November 1951
Morton, Private R.F., killed in action on 5 November 1951
Musgrove, Corporal R.F., killed in action on 4 November 1951
Munn, Sergeant A.R., killed in action on 4 November 1951
Price, Corporal T., killed in action on 4 November 1951
Rogers, Private J.H., killed in action on 5 November 1951

Smith, Private D., killed in action on 4 November 1951*
Sutherland, Sergeant B.J., killed in action on 5 November 1951 *
Wright, Private J., killed in action on 5 November 1951

The five men with an asterisk against their name were all members of The Argyll and Sutherland Highlanders, who were attached to the King's Own Scottish Borderers.

Because of the determined defensive action by the men of the Borderers, more than 1,000 Chinese troops of the attacking force were killed. Besides Bill Speakman's award of the Victoria Cross, 2nd Lieutenant William Purves, was awarded the Distinguished Service Order for his actions on Hill 217.

Chapter Four

Lieutenant Philip Kenneth Edward Curtis, VC

Philip Kenneth Edward Curtis, was born on 7 July 1926 in Plymouth, Devon, to Edward Curtis and his wife Ethel (née Richards).

With the Second World War in full swing, Philip Curtis, like most young men of his generation, was keen to sign up and do his bit for the war effort. In 1943, when he was just 17, he attempted to enlist in the Royal Air Force as he desperately wanted to be a pilot, but he was rejected due to his age. He eventually enlisted in the British Army in 1944 when he reached the age of 18, but he did not see active service in an overseas operational theatre of war, mainly due to the fact that by the time he had completed his basic training, the war was almost over.

At the war's end, and with no idea of what he would do back in civvy street, he opted to remain in the army; on 3 May 1946 he was given an emergency commission in the regular British Army with the Duke of Cornwall's Light Infantry, but due to circumstances he never actually got to serve with any of their battalions. He did however serve at the Headquarters Command in the Middle East, during which time he was attached to the Royal Army Service Corps. Demobbed in 1948, he was given the honorary rank of captain and placed on the officers' reserve list.

Philip Curtis married in April 1946 while serving in the army, when he was just 20 years of age. His bride, Joan Hayes from Devonport, Devon, died suddenly in September 1949, at the age of just 23. The couple had a daughter, Philippa Susan Curtis, who I believe was born sometime in 1947, and would have been no older than 2 when her mother died. Having checked the Civil Registration Marriage Index for England & Wales, for the period which covers 1916–2005, I believe Philippa may have married a man by the name of Griffin, in Plymouth in the Summer of 1968, and eventually used Susan as her first name.

After having been placed on the Army Reserve, Philip didn't immediately take to life back in civvy street, finding it boring in comparison to his time spent in the forces.

The Korean war began in 1950, the year following the death of his wife Joan. With the numbers of men in the British Army being a great deal lower than they had been at the end of the Second World War, those who were still on the Army Reserve found themselves receiving recall papers in the post.

Philip Curtis was one of them. But this was a problem for him as he was the single father of a young daughter, which was a big responsibility. Despite his undoubted love for Phillipa, the desire to rejoin the army was a strong one. He had not seen active service during the Second World War, and now he had the somewhat unexpected opportunity to properly test himself as a soldier in a war that would more than likely see him serving on the front line.

His mother-in-law, Mrs Beatrice Hayes, agreed to look after Philippa, allowing him to rejoin the army. He quickly made it known to his senior officers that he wished to be considered for duties in Korea, not wanting to miss out on active service for a second time. He got his way and sailed from England on 17 October 1950, but the ship's destination was Japan and not South Korea. Japan was still an occupied nation in 1950, in the shape of American forces, as well as the British Commonwealth Occupation Force, whose headquarters were at the port city of Kure, although they also had responsibility for the areas of Shimane, Yamaguchi, Tottori, Okayama, Hiroshima and Shikoku Island. There then followed a period of frustration for Philip Curtis, with the United Nations counter offensive already underway against the Communist forces of North Korea.

Once in Korea the time seemed to drag for Philip; in reality this probably had more to do with him believing he would be going straight in to action as soon as he arrived, and because that didn't happen he had become anxious. He was worried that with a United Nations offensive against the

North Koreans having already begun, he was going to miss out on active service once again.

Christmas 1950 came and went, as did the months of January and February, and still he had received no orders or information about when he was going to be sent to South Korea. On 3 March 1951, just over four months after arriving in Japan, he finally found himself in South Korea, as the lieutenant in charge of No.1 platoon, A Company, 1st Battalion, Gloucestershire Regiment. Little did he know that just over seven weeks later his life would be at an end, albeit in glorious fashion, with his bravery laid bare for all to see.

Over the course of 22 and 23 April 1951, while in command of No. 1 platoon, 1st Battalion, Gloucestershire Regiment, Philip led a counter-attack against Chinese-held positions. What the below citation fails to include is that one of the grenades which he had thrown moments before he was shot dead hit its intended target, totally destroying the enemy position, but sadly he never lived to see what he had achieved.

The following is an article taken from the Wikipedia page on Lieutenant Philip Kenneth Curtis, which is an account by Anthony Farrar-Hockley, an officer in the British Army, who served in the Battle of Imjin River, and witnessed the bravery which won Philip the Victoria Cross.

Phil is called to the telephone at this moment; Pat's voice sounds in his ear.

'Phil, at the present rate of casualties we can't hold on unless we get the Castle Site back. Their machine-guns up there completely dominate your platoon and most of Terry's. We shall never stop their advance until we hold that ground again.'

Phil looks over the edge of the trench at the Castle Site, two hundred yards away, as Pat continues talking, giving him the instructions for the counter attack. They talk for a minute or so; there is not much more to be said when an instruction is given to assault with a handful of tired men across open ground. Everyone knows it is vital: everyone knows it is appallingly dangerous.

The only details to be fixed are the arrangements for supporting fire; and, though A Company's Gunners are dead, Ronnie will support them from D Company's hill. Behind, the machine-gunners will ensure that they are not engaged from the open eastern flank. Phil gathers his tiny assault party together.

It is time, they rise from the ground and move forward to the barbed wire that once protected the rear of John's platoon. Already two men are hit and Papworth, the Medical Corporal, is attending to them. They are through the wire safely, safely! when the machine-gun in the bunker begins to fire. Phil is badly wounded: he drops to the ground. They drag him back through the wire somehow and seek what little cover there is as it creeps across their front. The machine-gun stops, content now it has driven them back; waiting for a better target when they move into the open again. 'It's all right, sir,' says someone to Phil. 'The Medical Corporal's been sent for. He'll be here any minute.'

Phil raises himself from the ground, rests on a friendly shoulder, then climbs by a great effort on to one knee. 'We must take the Castle Site,' he says; and gets up to take it. The others beg him to wait until his wounds are tended. One man places a hand on his side. 'Just wait until Papworth has seen you, sir.'

But Phil has gone: gone to the wire, gone through the wire, gone towards the bunker. The others come out behind him, their eyes all on him. And suddenly it seems as if, for a few breathless moments, the whole of the remainder of that field of battle is still and silent, watching amazed, the lone figure that runs so painfully forward to the bunker holding the approach to the Castle Site: one tiny figure, throwing grenades, firing a pistol, set to take Castle Hill.

Perhaps he will make it in spite of his wounds, in spite of the odds, perhaps this act of supreme gallantry may, by its sheer audacity, succeed. But the machine-gun in the bunker fires into him: he staggers, falls, and is dead instantly; the grenade he threw a second before his death explodes after it in the mouth of the bunker. The machine-gun does not fire on three of Phil's platoon who run forward to pick him up; it does not fire again through the battle: it is destroyed; the muzzle blown away, the crew dead.

There is nothing more powerful about reading a first-hand, eye-witness account of such event, rather than reading the same events from an official citation.

Lieutenant Curtis was buried at the United Nations Memorial Cemetery in Busan, South Korea's second most populated city after Seoul. His Victoria Cross is currently on display at the Duke of Cornwall's Light Infantry Museum in Bodmin, Cornwall.

The following information was released by the War Office on 1 December 1953 and includes the citation for the award of the Victoria Cross to Lieutenant Curtis.

The Queen has been graciously pleased to approve the posthumous award of the Victoria Cross to Lieutenant Philip Kenneth Edward Curtis The Duke of Cornwall's Light Infantry, attached The Gloucestershire Regiment, in recognition of gallant and distinguished services in Korea.

During the first phase of the Battle of the Imjin River on the night of 22nd/23rd April, 1951, 'A' Company, 1 Glosters, was heavily attacked by a large enemy force. By dawn on 23rd April, the enemy had secured a footing on the 'Castle Hill' site in very close proximity to No. 2 Platoon's position.

The Company Commander ordered No. 1 Platoon, under the command of Lieutenant Curtis, to carry out a counter attack with a view to dislodging the enemy from the position. Under the covering of medium machine guns, the counter attack, gallantly led by Lieutenant Curtis, gained initial success, but was held up by heavy fire and grenades.

Enemy from just below the crest of the hill were rushed to reinforce the position and a fierce fire-fight developed, grenades also being freely used by both sides in this close quarter engagement. Lieutenant Curtis ordered some of his men to give him covering fire while he himself rushed the main position of resistance; in this charge Lieutenant Curtis was severely wounded by a grenade. Several of his men crawled out and pulled him back under cover, but, recovering himself, Lieutenant Curtis insisted on making a second attempt. Breaking free from the men who wished to restrain him, he made another desperate charge, hurling grenades as he went, but was killed by a burst of fire when within a few yards of his objective.

Although the immediate objective of this counter-attack was not achieved, it had yet a great effect on the subsequent course of the battle; for although the enemy had gained a footing on a position vital to the defence of the whole company area, this success had resulted in such furious reaction that they made no further effort to exploit their success in this immediate area; had they done so, the eventual withdrawal of the company might well have proved impossible.

Lieutenant Curtis's conduct was magnificent throughout this bitter battle.

The above citation appeared in the *London Gazette*, 1 December 1953.

Curtis was recommended for the award of the Victoria Cross by his commanding officer, Lieutenant Colonel James Power Carne, who was also awarded the Victoria Cross for his actions during the same battle. Curtis's award of the Victoria Cross was the fourth and last of the Korean war.

Another article about Lieutenant Curtis also appeared in the press on Wednesday 2 December 1951, this time it was the turn of the *Northern Whig* newspaper to report his award of the Victoria Cross.

Wounded, he pressed on, Hurling Grenades.
VC for Officer who died in charge at Enemy.

The posthumous award of the Victoria Cross to a young lieutenant for 'magnificent conduct' in the Imjin River battle, announced last night, was recommended by Lieutenant-Colonel, J.P, Carne, commanding officer of the 1st Battalion, Gloucestershire Regiment, who also won the VC in the same Korean battle.

The lieutenant, Philip Kenneth Edward Curtis, aged 24, the Duke of Cornwall's Light Infantry, though severely wounded, charged the enemy, hurling grenades as he went, and was killed within a few yards of his objective.

Lieutenant Curtis's mother, a widow, lives in Pembroke Street, Devonport. Last night she told a reporter, 'Even as a boy Philip was fearless, and always eager to run messages for the wardens during the wartime raids on Plymouth.'

Lieutenant Curtis leaves an orphan daughter, his wife having died some years ago. The little girl is cared for by her maternal grandmother.

Remarkably it was more than three years after his death before the posthumous award of the Victoria Cross was presented to his mother, Florence, by Queen Elizabeth ll in an investiture at Buckingham Palace. Present with Florence, was Philip's daughter Philippa, and his mother-in-law, Mrs Beatrice Hayes. A bitter-sweet day that was filled with the sadness at their loved one's death, a thrill at meeting the Queen at Buckingham Palace, and a pride in the supreme bravery and gallantry which Philip displayed while leading his men in to battle against a determined and well-drilled enemy.

On the death of Florence Curtis, the medal was handed down to her daughter, Philippa, who, sometime in the early 1970s, sold the medal at auction at Sotheby's in London. It was purchased by a medal dealer, John Hayward, for the princely sum of £7,200, with the money being placed in a trust fund for her son, Philip, who had been named after his grandfather.

A short while later, John Hayward sold the Victoria Cross to the Duke of Cornwall Light Infantry's museum at Bodmin in Cornwall, whom he had outbid for the medal at auction, for £6,200. An extremely noble gesture.

Chapter Five

Lieutenant Colonel
James Power Carne, VC, DSO

James Power Carne was born on 11 April 1906, in Falmouth, Cornwall, to parents George Newby Carne, who worked as a brewer and wine merchant, and Annie Emily Le Poar Carne. Her maiden name was 'Power', hence the relevance of James's middle name.

Despite being born in Falmouth, James Power Carne spent much of his life living in Cranham, Surrey. On leaving school, and already having decided on a life in the military, the highly intelligent James entered the Imperial Service College at Windsor, before attending the Royal Military College at Sandhurst. On 3 September 1925, at the age of 19 and having successfully completed his officers' course he received a commission as a second lieutenant in the Gloucestershire Regiment. Exactly two years later he was further promoted to lieutenant, but it then took him eight more years to make it to captain. On 3 September 1942, during the course of the Second World War, he was promoted to major, and finally to lieutenant colonel on 7 February 1949, a promotion that was published in a supplement to the *London Gazette* newspaper of 8 March 1949.

On 25 June 1950, and with tensions in the region having been running high for some time, North Korean forces crossed the 38th parallel; in doing so they invaded neighbouring South Korea, and so started the Korean war.

At a meeting on 6 July 1950 in 10 Downing Street, the British government decided that they would not send military land forces to Korea. This was because at the time Britain had numerous other military commitments, which had resulted in her resources being stretched to the limits. They were already committed militarily in Malaysia due to the Malayan

Emergency, which was getting worse by the day. The French, who were heavily committed in Vietnam, were reliant on promised aid from Britain. Another real concern for the British government was the potential threat of a Chinese invasion of Hong Kong, because of the growing tensions in the region.

Such situations are always made worse by politics and what one country may or may not think about another. This was highlighted when South Korean and American troops, as part of the United Nations forces, began suffering set-backs in their fight against North Korea. The knock-on effect of this was the potential negative view of the United Kingdom as a world power, which it was at the time. Something which had to be pointed out by the Foreign Office before the British government reacted. There was also the worry that the relationship with the United States was in real danger of suffering long term damage if military support was not forthcoming, and quickly.

On 25 July 1950, at a hastily arranged Cabinet meeting, it was decided that British and Commonwealth land forces would in fact be sent to Korea, despite there being no change in the overseas commitments of British forces. So the rhetorical question is, what had occurred that had caused such a U-turn in government thinking? The very next day, Manny Shinwell, the Minister of Defence, made the following announcement in the House of Commons.

> Nonetheless, His Majesty's Government have no desire to escape their obligation to play their full part as a member of the United Nations in the restoration of order in Korea. It will not be easy for us to make forces available, but I can tell the House that we are today notifying the Secretary-General of the United Nations that we are prepared to send to that theatre, for use under the orders of the United Nations Commander, an effective land reinforcement which will be a self-contained force including infantry, armour, artillery and engineers, together with the administrative backing required to maintain it.

It was decided that the British Army's 29th Infantry Brigade, which would require reservists to be called up so that it was completely up to strength, would consist of the 1st Battalion, Royal Northumberland Fusiliers; the 1st Battalion, Gloucestershire Regiment; and the 1st Battalion, Royal Ulster Rifles. All three regiments were stationed throughout the United Kingdom, and initially were to be Britain's only commitment to the situation in Korea. But with a rapid escalation of the conflict, it was also decided to send further British forces in the form of the 27th Infantry Brigade, who were stationed in Hong Kong. This included the 1st Battalion, Middlesex Regiment; the 1st Battalion, Argyll and Sutherland Highlanders; and the 1st Battalion, Leicestershire Regiment. The downside of the 27th Infantry Brigade was that they would be totally reliant on the Americans for much of their equipment as they had absolutely no artillery at all, and little in the way of vehicles for transport. The announcement of these extra troops to be supplied to serve alongside the other forces of the United Nations was made in the House of Commons by the British government on 20 August 1950. In the end it was decided that the 1st Battalion, Leicestershire Regiment would remain behind in Hong Kong because of the potential threat from the Chinese authorities. The concern was that if it became common knowledge that Hong Kong had, in essence, been left undefended by the British, this might be the encouragement China needed to invade it.

From a United Nations perspective, there was understandably an urgency involved in arranging for the British forces to arrive in Korea as soon as possible. The men of the Middlesex Regiment and the Argyll and Sutherland Highlanders would be somewhat delayed, as between the time of the decision to deploy them to Korea being made and the time of the message reaching their units, all the men had been given leave on the Friday night and had headed into Hong Kong City after a busy and hectic week. The chances of all these men returning sober to their barracks was extremely slim to say the least, and many would be so drunk that they would return several hours late. The likelihood was that the two regiments would not be able to leave for Korea until the Monday morning at the earliest.

There were two other immediate problems for both the Gloucestershire Regiment and The Argyll and Sutherland Highlanders. First, both were under strength and the British government had decided at the eleventh hour that men under the age of 19 from either regiment would not be sent to Korea, as they didn't want them serving in combat at such an age. This meant suitable replacements had to be found from other units at extremely short notice; in fairness, this is part of the reality of any war – nothing ever runs smoothly.

The man who had been put in charge of the 27th Infantry Brigade, Coad, arrived in Puscan, South Korea by air on 27 August 1950, while the men of the Gloucestershire Regiment and the Argyll and Sutherland Highlanders arrived by sea on board the Royal Navy aircraft carrier, HMS *Unicorn* and the cruiser HMS *Ceylon*, which arrived in Korea on 29 August. On 3 September 1950, just four days after arriving in the country, elements of the brigade went into action as part of the defence of the Pusan Perimeter, but just two days later they were moved to the front line along a section of the Naktong River, just south-west of Taegu.

Captain Neil Buchanan and Private Tam Taylor of the Argyll and Sutherland Highlanders, along with Private Reginald Streeter of the Middlesex Regiment, became the Brigade's first casualties of the war.

It was a further five months, in November 1950, before the 45-year-old Carne, and the 1st Battalion, the Gloucestershire Regiment, of which he was the commanding officer, were attached to the British Army's 29th Independent Infantry brigade, and sent out to Korea as part of the United Nations forces supporting South Korea.

It wasn't long before Carne and his battalion were in the thick of the action. The Battle of Ch'ongch'on River took place over an eight-day period between 25 November and 2 December 1950, and saw Chinese forces pitted against a combined United Nations force consisting of American, South Korean, Turkish, Australian, British, Canadian, Indian and New Zealand troops.

The battle resulted in a decisive Chinese victory which saw all areas north of the 38th parallel in the control of Communist forces, and all United Nations forces back behind the same line.

In the aftermath of the defeat of the United Nations forces, it was the job of Lieutenant Colonel Carne and his men to provide a rearguard action for these retreating forces.

Somewhat ironically, it was the initial successes of United Nations forces with the landings at Inchon, the breakout from the Pusan Perimeter, and the destruction of the Communist forces of the Korean People's Army during September 1950 that brought China in to the conflict, as the United Nations forces quickly pushed on to the Chinese-North Korean Border.

Concerned by the speed of the United Nations advance through North Korea, the Communist government of China decided that they had to act. Mao Zedong, the Chinese leader, launched his first phase response to the advances of the United Nations forces by sending his troops into North Korea on 25 October 1950. It took elements of the Chinese People's Volunteer Army just eleven days to push United Nations forces all the way back to the Ch'ongch'on River. The same Chinese forces then became victims of their own success, because on 5 November 1950 they had to halt their advance, not because of a lack of manpower but because of logistics concerning ammunition, food and water.

The halt of the advance, which in certain areas also resulted in the withdrawal of Chinese forces, was totally misinterpreted by United Nations planners. They made two incorrect assumptions. First, they took the halt to mean that the Chinese involvement in Korea would not be on a large scale, and second, they estimated that there were only somewhere in the region of 30,000 Chinese troops in North Korea, when in reality there were six times that amount. A significant and potentially costly mistake on the part of the United Nations planners.

Lieutenant Colonel Carne was also in command of the 1st Battalion, the Gloucestershire Regiment on 16 February 1951, when they were part of a successful United Nations counter offensive against enemy forces south of the River Han.

On the night of 22/23 April 1951, Lieutenant Colonel Carne was present when his men came under heavy enemy attack at the Battle of

Imjin River, in North Korea. The battalion survived the onslaught, having managed to repulse the enemy's attack, but in doing so they sustained heavy casualties.

For the three days between 23 and 25 April 1951, the men of Carne's 1st Battalion, came under heavy and almost continuous attack, by a much larger and heavily motivated enemy force, sustaining more heavy casualties in the process. It wasn't just one attack they fought off, but a repeated number of mass attacks, some of which came very close to the Gloucestershire's defensive positions.

Men of the Regiment's 1st Battalion were totally cut off from the rest of the Brigade during 24 and 25 April, but did not surrender or try to escape; instead they held firm as an effective fighting unit to keep the enemy at bay. With a totally different mindset, the Chinese, who appeared to have little or no regard for human life, threw their men forward in wave upon wave, content in the knowledge that eventually they would overcome the British defenders, no matter how many of their men became casualties.

Throughout all of this furore, Lieutenant Colonel Carne was calmness personified. If he was afraid, he did not show any fear. He must have been a fantastic inspiration for the officers and men who served under him, and if they had any doubts, which many of them would have, they had to look no further than the eyes of their own commanding officer for the reassurance they would have so badly needed.

While speaking to the Brigade's commander over the radio, Lieutenant Colonel Carne told a bit of a white lie when he informed his boss that everything was fine, that they could hold on, and that the men were in good heart, even though the reality of the situation was somewhat different.

Lieutenant Colonel Carne knew that no matter what happened, he had to keep his men in a calm but determined manner, ready and able to deal with each and every one of the enemy's attacks. With apparent total disregard for his own personal safety he continually tried to rally his men. While under continuous mortar and machine-gun fire, he moved among his officers and men in an attempt to keep up their morale, despite knowing the precarious position they were all in. He reasoned that if his men could see that not only was he not afraid, but that he appeared confident and cheery, then his disposition would rub off on them.

During this prolonged period of battle, the overriding trait displayed by Lieutenant Colonel Carne, was that of true leadership. For him, his place was with his men, leading them from the front, not in the safety of a rear position where he could bark out orders over a radio without knowing the full facts of what was unfolding. Despite holding the high rank of an officer he was, first and foremost, a soldier who knew how to do things in a hands-on practical sense; he did not have to rely on the pages of a text book on military tactics. Rather than leave it to more junior officers, in both rank and age, he was more than happy to lead from the front. There were at least two occasions when, armed with grenades and a rifle, he led small counter attacks, which not only successfully stopped the enemy attacks, but also forced them to retreat. Each time preventing some of their defensive positions from being overrun.

His excellent leadership, his undoubted courage and his coolness of head were there for all of his officers and men to see. He was no doubt an inspiration for all of them; for some, this would have made the difference between staying alive or being killed by a determined enemy. 'He fully realised that his flanks had been turned, but he also knew that the abandonment of his position would clear the way for the enemy to make a major breakthrough and this would have endangered the Corps.' (*London Gazette*, 23 October 1953)

Eventually it became apparent that the position he and his men had so bravely and valiantly fought to defend had become untenable, with little or no hope of being relieved. With this in mind, they were ordered to pull back. Rather than give the order that it was every man for himself, Carne didn't panic in the face of adversity, but instead delved deeply in to his bag of 'how to think clearly while in a difficult situation' options, and remained calm. He split his battalion in to smaller groups, each under the command of an officer, and one at a time he had them pull back and return to the comparative safety of their rear lines. Lieutenant Colonel Carne led the last of the groups in their escape attempts, but after nearly a day on their feet,

Carne and the remainder of his men were captured by the Chinese and taken as prisoners of war. He spent the next nineteen months of his life in solitary confinement in a PoW camp in North Korea, before eventually being released in September 1953. Over the course of those few days in April 1951, some 600 officers and men were killed in the fight against the North Korean forces.

The citation for the award of his Distinguished Service Order appeared in the *London Gazette*:

> The War Office 13 July 1951
> The King has been graciously pleased to approve the following award in recognition of gallant and distinguished service in Korea.
> Lieutenant Colonel (33647) James Power Carne. The Gloucestershire Regiment. (Missing).

It was interesting to note that at the time of the announcement of the award of his Distinguished Service Order, the British authorities still had no idea if Lieutenant Colonel Carne was alive or dead. The other comment worth making here is that it would appear the award of his Distinguished Service Order was for his action during the Battle of Imjin River in April 1951, after which he spent the rest of the war as a prisoner in captivity in North Korea. This is somewhat strange, as the award for his Victoria Cross was for the exact same action. This then begs the question: why weren't the other three recipients of the Victoria Cross during the Korean war also awarded the Distinguished Service Order?

Carne also had another honour bestowed on him in 1951, as reported in the *Western Mail* of Monday 31 December:

> Lieut-Col. James Power Carne, DSO, commanding officer of the 1st Battalion the Gloucestershire Regiment at the Battle of Imjin River in Korea, is to receive the honorary freedom of Gloucester. A resolution to confer the honour upon Lieut-Col. Carne, will be submitted to the city council at a special meeting on Wednesday.

Names of one officer and 110 other ranks are listed in a War Office statement released in London on Saturday as having been identified as prisoners of war in the hands of Chinese Communists in Korea. Only 14 of them, all Gloucesters, had not previously been known to be prisoners.

On 27 October 1953, Carne was awarded the Victoria Cross; the final two paragraphs of the citation for the award appeared in the *London Gazette* on that day:

Lieutenant Colonel Carne showed powers of leadership which can seldom have been surpassed in the history of our Army.

He inspired his officers and men to fight beyond the normal limits of human endurance, in spite of overwhelming odds and ever increasing casualties, shortage of ammunition and water.

On 30 October 1953, he was also awarded the Distinguished Service Cross by the Americans, which is the second highest military award that can be given to a member of the United States Army, and by approval of the President of the United States of America, it can also be conferred on soldiers of foreign nations. Lieutenant Colonel Carne's award came about for his gallant and distinguished services during operations by forces of the United Nations in Korea.

The citation for this award appeared in the *London Gazette*:

The War Office 30th October 1953

The Queen has been pleased to grant unrestricted permission for the wearing of the following decorations which have been conferred on the undermentioned personnel in recognition of gallant and distinguished services during operations by the United Nations in Korea:-

Decoration conferred by the President of the United States of America.

Distinguished Service Cross
Lieutenant Colonel 33647 James Power Carne, VC, DSO,
The Gloucestershire Regiment.

It was awarded for extreme gallantry and risk of life in actual combat with an armed enemy force. Such actions that merit the Distinguished Service Cross must be of such a high degree that they are above those required for all other United States combat decorations, but do not meet the criteria for the Medal of Honour, which is the highest possible military award obtainable in the American military. The Distinguished Service Cross was first awarded during the First World War.

On 4 July 2015, it was announced that Lieutenant Colonel James Power Carne was to be commemorated on a South Korean stamp, to commemorate the 65th anniversary of the beginning of the Korean war.

Chapter Six

Major Kenneth Muir, VC

As the Communist masses smashed their way across the 38th parallel and into South Korea, causing the meagre forces of the United Nations to retreat, they provided a reminder of an early phase of what was, after all, a fluctuating campaign.

The primary tactic of the North Korean and Chinese forces appears to have been nothing more taxing than the utilisation of a large number of troops to attack any one position, with no apparent care or concern at the number of men they lost in doing so.

The Argyll and Sutherland Highlanders were one of the British Regiments sent to Korea as part of the United Nations commitment in the region, and part of their deployment saw them utilised in an attempt to drive the North Koreans back beyond the 38th parallel.

The circumstances in which Major Kenneth Muir was awarded his Victoria Cross is a battle episode that adds to the lustre of the Argyll and Sutherland Highlanders, and will have an honoured place in the annals of their achievements.

Such events also show that the United Nations simply did not have adequate ground forces in place in Korea to deal effectively with the large number of Communist forces they were up against. It soon become apparent that the Korean war was not going to be a quick fix, and bringing it to an acceptable conclusion was going to be just as difficult.

Having sent ground troops into Korea, the United Nations found themselves in an extremely difficult situation. They could not now withdraw those troops, nor allow themselves to be defeated because this would cause not only a massive loss of face in political terms, they would also be as good as handing South Korea over to the Communist North. This left two possible alternatives for the United Nations: have their member countries send more troops to the region to counter the large number of Communist forces, which would ultimately just lead to more deaths, or sit down around a table and agree a way forward that would not require thousands more young men to lose their lives. After a further three years of fighting and thousands more deaths on both sides, the latter of the two options finally took place, with hostilities coming to an end on 27 July 1953. The boundary remained in place on the 38th parallel and, seventy-seven years later, still is.

Kenneth Muir was born in Scotland in 1912, the son of Lieutenant Colonel J.W. Muir, who in the early 1920s was the commanding officer of the depot at Stirling Castle. Between 1924 and 1927 he was in command of the 1st Battalion, Argyll and Sutherland Highlanders while they were stationed in Egypt.

Kenneth followed in his father's footsteps and decided on a life in the military. As a 19-year-old he attended Sandhurst Military College (subsequently the Royal Military Academy Sandhurst) where, having successfully completed and passed his course in 1932, he was commissioned as a First Lieutenant with the 1st Battalion, Argyll and Sutherland Highlanders, the old 93rd (Sutherland Highlanders) Regiment of Foot, before transferring to the Regiment's 1st Battalion later the same year. He went with them when they were sent out to India, where they remained until after the outbreak of the Second World War. After the desert campaign, he took command of a company of the Regiment's 7th (Stirling County) Battalion, and served with them in Messina, Sicily.

On his return from the North African campaign in 1943, he initially remained with the 7th Battalion, before taking up a staff position in February 1944. While in this role he was sent to America where he was stationed in Washington as a liaison officer and remained there to the end of the war. He was then sent out to post-war Germany where he took command of the reconstituted 2nd Battalion, but he was only there for a few months before he returned to England to take up a staff appointment at the War Office in London. He remained there for the next five years before being sent out to Korea in 1950 with the 1st Battalion.

Having left Hong Kong on Sunday 20 August 1950 and endured a nine-day voyage across the South and East China Seas, the 27th British

Infantry Brigade arrived in Korea on Tuesday 29 August 1950, with men from the Middlesex Regiment on board the aircraft carrier HMS *Unicorn*, while those from the Argyll and Sutherland Highlanders were on board the cruiser, HMS *Ceylon*. The Royal Navy vessels had been accompanied on their journey from Hong Kong by the Australian destroyers HMAS *Warramunga* and HMAS *Bataan*.

It was a warm sunny morning, with nothing more strenuous than a gentle breeze accompanied by clear blue skies as the men of the 1st Battalion, Middlesex Regiment, and 1st Battalion, Argyll and Sutherland Highlanders stepped on to the quayside of Pusan harbour. It was their first time in Korea.

There was no rush to disembark; in fact it was more than an hour after both vessels had tied up and switched off their powerful engines, that the first man came ashore, to be met by crowds of grateful South Korean civilians and some inquisitive dock workers. Scottish pipers of the Argyll and Sutherland Highlanders provided the stirring sound that only bagpipes can make.

The British contingent became the first non-American troops to join the United Nations forces in Korea. It was hard to believe there was a war going on with all the pomp and ceremony. A South Korean band and choir played and sang, 'God save the King' as the Union Jack was raised on Korean soil.

Then it was the turn of an American military band to join in the fun. They started off by playing the 'St Louis Blues' and finished with 'Colonel Bogey', which brought smiles and laughter from the disembarking British troops.

The first man ashore was from neither regiment. That honour went to Leading Seaman Brian Davey of Ivybridge, South Devon. The first soldier to get ashore was Regimental Sergeant Major Boyde of The Argyll and Sutherland Highlanders, who was from Dunbartonshire; he provided the somewhat reassuring news to waiting reporters, that he was looking forward to the idea of fighting in Korea.

The first officer was Major Gwyn of the Middlesex Regiment, but when Major Muir landed, a young South Korean girl ran up to him, bowed, and handed him a bouquet of flowers, not the normal adornment a soldier of the time would have wished to be seen holding. But being both an officer and a gentleman, he took the flowers in his arms, stood to attention and threw up his best salute. Seeing the respectful response afforded by Major Muir, more young girls suddenly darted from the waiting crowds and handed similar offerings to the major's slightly embarrassed but appreciative soldiers.

Also waiting on the dock to greet the newly arrived British contingent to the United Nations forces was Brigadier B.A. Coad, the commander of the 1st Battalion, Argyll and Sutherland Highlanders. Earlier, he had also been presented with a bouquet of flowers by a young South Korean girl, which was immediately met by a salvo of whistling from the troops on the ships. After that the flowers were quickly handed over to an officer standing next to him – so quickly in fact that he practically threw them.

Although several officers from the Argyll and Sutherland Highlanders were wearing their kilts on the quayside, the expectation for both officers and men deployed in fighting zones was to be in full battledress.

Brigadier Coad was accompanied by the commanding officer of the 1st Battalion, Middlesex Regiment, Lieutenant Colonel A.M. Man, along with a number of other British, American and South Korean officials.

The British forces had their own arms, ammunition and tea, but were reliant on the Americans for food in the form of US Army rations. Not necessarily to the liking of the more discerning of palates, but needs must.

It was noted by observers of the occasion that the British troops acted in a much more disciplined and strict manner than their American counterparts had done earlier that day. The British soldiers were dressed in jungle green uniforms, tan berets and were carrying full field packs and a combination of rifles and automatic weapons. Their morale was a positive one, and they were keen to get on with the job in hand, as was confirmed when a couple of their number spoke with gathered members of the Press. Company Sergeant Major Robert Murray said: 'We're quite happy. We can handle the mountain fighting. We have always taken it, so we can carry on.' While Lance Corporal Charles Bell, who had been a coal miner before enlisting in the army, said: 'We'll have a go at them, sure thing.' Not the most eloquent of replies, but both men who were serving with the Argyll and Sutherland Highlanders, adequately made their point.

The 27th British Infantry Division was involved in the defence of the Pusan Perimeter, a battle fought between North Korean forces and the United Nations Command. It was one of the Korean war's first major engagements and one which saw the United Nations forces pushed back to what was known as the 'Pusan Perimeter', a defensive line which stretched some 140 miles around the south-eastern tip of South Korea, which included the port of Busan. The United Nations forces included those from South Korea, the United States as well as the United Kingdom.

Despite North Korean forces' repeated attempts at breaking through the United Nations defensive lines, they were not successful. The port at Busan proved to be a major advantage to the United Nations forces, who were able to bring in reinforcements, ammunition, food and medical supplies, along with equipment, to help them sustain against a determined and dogged enemy.

The longer the fighting continued, the bigger the swing was away from the Korean People's Army, who became hampered by enormous casualties and overstretched supply lines. At the start of the fighting at the Battle of Pusan Perimeter, the North Koreans had a force estimated to have been some 98,000 in number, of which 70,000 were combat troops. By the time the fighting at Pusan was over, they had sustained a total of 63,590 casualties. Having incurred such losses it is no wonder the Korean People's Army had to begin its retreat on 15 September 1950, as United Nations forces began a counter attack the same day at Inchon.

The mindset of the North Korean leaders and their military commanders at that time is hard to fathom. Despite the obvious fact that whatever tactics they were deploying were ineffective, it must also have been clear that their losses were not sustainable for any protracted period of time, and long before they eventually decided to retreat. To my mind, it shows a total disregard for the lives and wellbeing of their own troops.

Most Allied military leaders would have accepted that their position was untenable and retreated long before the Koreans eventually did, because they would have been more considerate to the needs of their men, especially the wounded.

On 22 September 1950, as part of the American 24th Infantry Division, the British 27th Infantry Brigade were really brought in to play; they were tasked with protecting the Americans' left flank as they advanced during the Pusan Perimeter counter-attack. Six days later, on 22 September, near the town of Songu, situated north of the Naktong River, the Argyll and Sutherland Highlanders were in action defending a major road junction on a route into the South Korean capital of Seoul.

By the following day there had been a number of United Nations casualties, and problems had arisen in the ability to evacuate them. During that same day Major Muir arrived with a stretcher party detail to assist and speed up the process of evacuating the wounded, but as is the case in war, any given situation doesn't stay the same for long, and the events near Songju on 23 September 1950 were no different.

In the early hours of 23 September, 'B' and 'C' Companies of the 1st Battalion, Argyll and Sutherland Highlanders, swarmed up the steep 900ft of Hill 282, taking the breakfasting enemy troops by surprise, and forced them off the top. The euphoric feeling of victory soon dissipated when it quickly became apparent that their position was being overlooked by enemy forces on the higher Hill 388, which was nearly a mile away to the south-west, but which still dominated their position. It wasn't long before they counter-attacked in large numbers, and despite the density of the shrub, the speed of their attack was not affected. The North Koreans supported their infantry with artillery and mortar fire, which quickly found its mark and began landing on the British position. American artillery units had already been withdrawn from the area, and the available American tanks could play no part in defending the British troops because of the steepness of the immediate terrain.

Just after noon, and realising that if the enemy artillery continued to bombard their position they wouldn't be able to hang out much longer,

Major Muir called in an airstrike. This resulted in the arrival of three P-51 Mustangs of the United States Air Force, 18th Fighter Bomber Wing, a short while later. Their intended target was the North Korean 'Hill 388'. The Argyll and Sutherland Highlanders, in keeping with such situations, displayed white recognition markers which indicated to the incoming aircraft that their location was occupied by friendly forces. The North Koreans, on seeing the British put out their white markers, quickly realised there was about to be an airstrike on their position, so they copied the British move and covered their location with similar white recognition markers. This caused confusion among the American pilots who, understandably, did not know where to drop their bombs. The situation was made worse when the tactical air control party were unable to make radio contact with any of the P-51 Mustang aircraft. But suddenly, inexplicably and without any warning, the American aircraft dropped their napalm bombs on Hill 282 and the Argyll and Sutherland Highlanders troops who were defending the position. As if that wasn't bad enough, they then strafed the same area with .50 calibre machine-gun fire. From start to finish the attack lasted just two minutes.

Those who had survived the attack had to quickly make their way down the hill to escape the burning napalm which covered much of the crest of the hill. Major Muir, who had early been at the top delivering much needed ammunition, had been at the bottom of the hill at the time of the attack. Looking back up to the crest of the hill, through the dispersing flames, he noticed that some of his men were still alive. Not knowing if they were wounded or able-bodied, he quickly gathered a group of men and made his way back up the hill.

While the evacuation of the wounded was under way, North Korean forces launched a series of attacks on the position, and it became apparent that the United Nations forces were in danger of being overrun. But it was almost a pyrrhic victory, because having regained the position, they now had to hold it, and with their dwindling numbers, that was never going to be a straightforward task. Major Muir wanted to be able to hold the position long enough for all the wounded to be safely evacuated.

While doing so, and personally engaging the enemy with a mortar, he was fatally wounded.

In November 1950 the United Nations command announced that Major Kenneth Muir had been posthumously awarded a Silver Star for the gallantry which he displayed in action in which he was killed. For his actions on what was designated by the United Nations as Hill 282, Major Muir was awarded the Victoria Cross, the announcement of which was made on 6 January 1951, by which time he had also been awarded the Distinguished Service Cross by the United States, who had announced their award in November 1950.

Below is the citation for the award of the Victoria Cross, which appeared in the *London Gazette* on 5 January 1951.

On 23rd September, 1950, 'B' and 'C' Companies of the 1st Battalion, the Argyll and Sutherland Highlanders attacked an enemy-held feature, Hill 282, and by 0800 hrs had consolidated upon it.

Some difficulty was experienced in evacuating the wounded from the position and demands were made for stretcher-bearing parties to be sent forward by the Argyll and Sutherland Highlanders. At this juncture the position came under mortar and shell fire.

At approximately 0900 hrs. a stretcher-bearing party arrived and with it came the Argyll and Sutherland Highlanders' Second-in-Command, Major K Muir. He proceeded to organise the evacuation of the casualties.

At approximately 0930 hrs. small parties of the enemy started to infiltrate on the left flank, necessitating the reinforcing of the forward platoon. For the next hour this infiltration increased, as did the shelling and mortaring, causing further casualties within the two companies.

By 1100 hrs. casualties were moderately severe and some difficulty was being experienced in holding the enemy. In addition due to reinforcing the left flank and to providing personnel to assist with the wounded, both companies were so inextricably mixed that it was obvious that they must come under a unified command. Major Muir, although only visiting the position, automatically took over command and with complete disregard for his own personal safety started to move around the forward elements, cheering on and encouraging the men to greater efforts despite the fact that ammunition was running low. He was continually under enemy fire, and, despite entreaties from officers and men alike, refused to take cover.

An air-strike against the enemy was arranged and air recognition panels were put out on the ground. At approximately 1215 hrs. the air-strike came in, but unfortunately the aircraft hit the companies' position instead of that of the enemy. The main defensive position was hit with fire bombs and machine-gun fire, causing more casualties and necessitating the withdrawal of the remaining troops to a position some 50ft below the crest. There is no doubt that a complete retreat from the hill would have been fully justified at this time. Only some thirty fighting men remained and ammunition was extremely low. Major Muir, however, realised that the enemy had not taken immediate advantage of the unfortunate incident and that the crest was still unoccupied although under fire.

With the assistance of the three remaining officers, he immediately formed a small force of some thirty all ranks and personally led a counter attack on the crest. To appreciate fully the implication of this, it is necessary to realise how demoralising the effect of the air-strike had been and it was entirely due to the courage, determination and splendid example of this officer that such a counter-attack was possible. All ranks responded magnificently and the crest was retaken.

From this moment on, Major Muir's actions were beyond all possible praise. He was determined that the wounded would have adequate time to be taken out and he was just as determined that the enemy would not take the crest. Grossly outnumbered and under heavy automatic fire, Major Muir moved about his small force, redistributing fast diminishing ammunition, and when the ammunition for his own weapon was spent, he took over a 2-inch mortar, which he used with great effect against the enemy. While fixing the mortar he was still shouting encouragements and advice to his men, and for a further five minutes the enemy were held. Finally Major Muir was hit with two bursts of automatic fire which mortally wounded him, but even then he retained consciousness and was still as determined to fight on. His last words were: 'The Gooks will never drive the Argylls off this hill.'

The effect of his splendid leadership on the men was nothing short of amazing and it was entirely due to his magnificent courage and example and the spirit which he imbued in those about him that all wounded were evacuated from the hill, and, as was subsequently discovered, very heavy casualties inflicted on the enemy in defence of the crest.

It is quite amazing when you read such an account, which, I might add, is not uncommon with citations for the award of the Victoria Cross. As much as such actions are about bravery, gallantry and a steely determination not to be overcome, it is as though the individuals concerned get to a point of realisation where they become totally fixated on the job at hand and block out everything else, including what must be the obvious realisation that either the feat they have taken on is insurmountable, or there is a real danger that they are not going to survive the encounter. But, for the greater good of their comrades, they continue on; regardless of the outcome, the options of which they have fully considered, deciding instead to put their destiny – and their lives – in the hands of their Maker.

This very small and unique band of men do not shy away from danger, instead they fully embrace it and run towards it with a singular belief that in meeting the threat posed head on, they will overcome, in the hope and belief that their actions will save the lives of countless others of their comrades.

As an aside, The *Hartlepool Northern Daily Mail*, included an interesting, yet somewhat unusual, article among its pages on Saturday 6 January 1951:

> One of three children, two boys and a girl, born to a 32-year-old miner's wife, Mrs Marion Robertson, of Burnside Road, Menstrie, Clackmannanshire, in Stirling Royal Infirmary today, may be given the name of Major Kenneth Muir, Korea's first VC.
>
> The triplets were born within an hour of each other, and are reported to be doing well. Mrs Robertson has five other children aged between two and eleven years of age.
>
> When she sat up in bed this morning she read about the posthumous award of the Victoria Cross to Major Muir. A friend who visited her said that Major Muir's name was being considered for one of the boys.

On 14 February 1951, Major Muir's parents, Colonel and Mrs Muir, travelled to London for the bittersweet occasion of the investiture of their son's Victoria Cross at Buckingham Palace by King George VI. This wasn't the end of the story for the Muir family however. Tragically, on 14 April 1954, Colonel Muir committed suicide; it was said that he had done so due to never quite getting over his son's death. The following article appeared in the *Yorkshire Post and Leeds Intelligencer* on Wednesday 21 April 1954:

> Depressed by the death in 1950 of his son, who was posthumously awarded the first VC of the Korean war, Lieutenant Colonel G.W. Muir, stabbed himself with a knife and a pair of scissors 'in a frenzy of despair or in a maniacal outburst' it was stated at a Guildford inquest yesterday.
>
> Colonel Muir, aged 79, was a former commander of the 1st Battalion, the Argyll and Sutherland Highlanders, and it was when serving with the same battalion that his 38-year-old son,

Major Kenneth Muir, won the VC. The Major's last words were, 'The Gooks will never drive the Argylls off this hill.'

His father died in hospital after an operation for a fractured thigh the day after he had been found in his hotel room at Frimley, Surrey, with neck and stomach wounds.

Dr David Haler, pathologist, said that death was due to the shock of the wounds and the operation on the thigh, which was properly carried out.

The wounds were indicative of having been self-inflicted in a frenzy of despair or in a maniacal outburst.

The article continued:

Mrs Mary Godman, Colonel Muir's daughter, said that he had been separated from his wife for four years. He was very depressed because Major Muir was killed in Korea.

The coroner in the case, Mr J.F. Brown, stated that he would record, 'with the greatest reluctance', a verdict of 'suicide while of unbalanced mind'.

Silver and Bronze Stars

On Wednesday 22 November 1950 it was announced in a number of British newspapers, including the *Western Mail*, that the United Nations command, which at the time was situated in Tokyo, had announced the awards of three posthumous Silver Stars and five Bronze Stars, one of which was posthumous, to men serving with the 1st Battalion, Argyll and Sutherland Highlanders, for acts of gallantry and heroism carried out during the course of their involvement in the Korean war.

The awards were specifically made for a battle which took place near Songju, which is south west of Waegwan, on 23rd September 1950. The posthumous silver stars were awarded to Major Kenneth Muir, Second Lieutenant M.D.W. Buchannan, and Private E. Hill. The Bronze Sar, which was also awarded posthumously, went to Sergeant E. Pigg. Four other awards of the Bronze Star were also made to Lance Corporal J. Fairhurst, Lance Corporal H. Ward, Sergeant J. O'Sullivan, and Private W. Watts.

Below is a summary of the citations for each of those awards:

Lieutenant Buchannan. He led his platoon in a dawn assault on the crest of a prominent and strategic hill occupied by the enemy. Under heavy and close range fire from the enemy, the brave personal efforts and courageous leadership of Lieutenant Buchannan, together with his utter disregard for danger, materially assisted in the capture and subsequent consolidation of the entire hill objective.

During the fierce fighting Lieutenant Buchannan received mortal wounds, but continued to lead his platoon to the end of the action, when he then collapsed and died.

Private Hill. He distinguished himself by gallantry in the same action. He at all times demonstrated exceptional fighting ability and fearless aggressiveness, his exemplary valour, tenacious determination and disregard for personal danger uphold the highest traditions of military service.

Major Muir. The second-in-command of the battalion personally led companies 'B' and 'C' in the assault. His fearless personal example and superb leadership, together with his total disregard for danger under heavy and close range fire from the enemy, contributed greatly to the capture of the significant hill objective.

During a counter-attack by the enemy, Major Muir was seen standing alone on the hill's crest, single-handedly firing a two-inch mortar against the enemy, in order to cover a withdrawal.

It was during this gallant and intrepid action that he was mortally wounded and fell dead beside his weapon.

Sergeant Pigg. He took a conspicuous part in the capture of the hill crest. During the enemy's counter-attack he at all times demonstrated valour, determination, courage and a personal disregard for danger.

Lance Corporal Fairhurst. He was severely wounded in the action. The citation mentions his fearless example of extraordinary determination and his display of superb personal courage in the face of heavy enemy fire.

Lieutenant-Colonel James Power Carne, DSO VC. He was awarded the Victoria Cross for his actions in the Battle of Imjin River, during which he led **The Glorious Glosters** *in a famous stand against an overwhelming Chinese attack.*

Men from the King's Own Scottish Borderers in Korea.

Kenneth Muir, VC. He was awarded the Victoria Cross for his actions on 23 September 1950. The award was a posthumous one.

HILL 282   KOREA

Major
Kenneth MUIR
VC
Argyll and Sutherland Highlanders
23rd September 1950

FOR VALOUR

A memorial to Kenneth Muir, VC.

P/50980 MAJOR
K. MUIR, V.C.
THE ARGYLL AND SUTHERLAND
HIGHLANDERS
23RD SEPTEMBER 1950 AGE 38

Above: *Memorial for Kenneth Muir, VC.*

Right: *Bill Speakman, VC, in Korea.*

Left: *Bill Speakman arriving back in Korea after being in hospital in Japan.*

Below: *Bill Speakman with his mother after having received his Victoria Cross at Buckingham Palace*

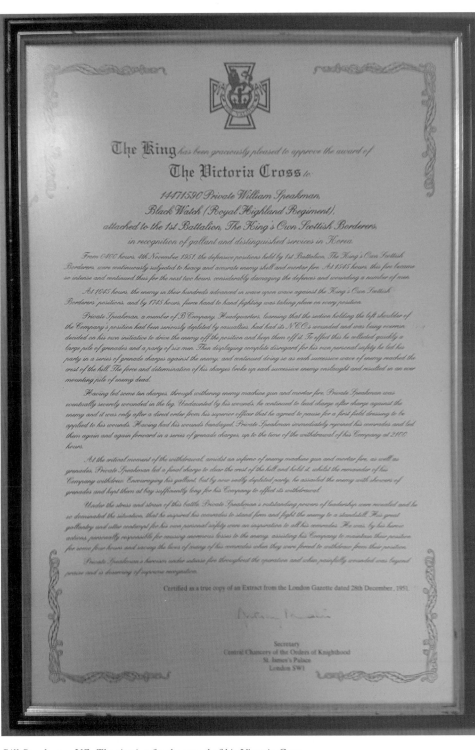

The King *has been graciously pleased to approve the award of*

The Victoria Cross *to*

14471590 Private William Speakman,

Black Watch (Royal Highland Regiment),

attached to the 1st Battalion, The King's Own Scottish Borderers,

in recognition of gallant and distinguished services in Korea.

From 0400 hours, 4th November 1951, the defensive positions held by 1st Battalion, The King's Own Scottish Borderers, were continuously subjected to heavy and accurate enemy shell and mortar fire. At 1545 hours, this fire became so intense and continued thus for the next two hours, considerably damaging the defences and wounding a number of men.

At 1645 hours, the enemy in their hundreds advanced in wave upon wave against the King's Own Scottish Borderers' positions, and by 1745 hours, fierce hand to hand fighting was taking place on every position.

Private Speakman, a member of B Company, Headquarters, learning that the section holding the left shoulder of the Company's position had been seriously depleted by casualties, had had its N.C.O's wounded and was being overrun, decided on his own initiative to drive the enemy off the position and keep them off it. To effect this he collected quickly a large pile of grenades and a party of six men. Then displaying complete disregard for his own personal safety he led his party in a series of grenade charges against the enemy, and continued doing so as each successive wave of enemy reached the crest of the hill. The force and determination of his charges broke up each successive enemy onslaught and resulted in an ever mounting pile of enemy dead.

Having led some ten charges, through withering enemy machine gun and mortar fire, Private Speakman was eventually severely wounded in the leg. Undaunted by his wounds, he continued to lead charge after charge against the enemy and it was only after a direct order from his superior officer that he agreed to pause for a first field dressing to be applied to his wounds. Having had his wounds bandaged, Private Speakman immediately rejoined his comrades and led them again and again forward in a series of grenade charges, up to the time of the withdrawal of his Company at 2100 hours.

At the critical moment of the withdrawal, amidst an inferno of enemy machine gun and mortar fire, as well as grenades, Private Speakman led a final charge to clear the crest of the hill and hold it, whilst the remainder of his Company withdrew. Encouraging his gallant, but by now sadly depleted party, he assailed the enemy with showers of grenades and kept them at bay sufficiently long for his Company to effect its withdrawal.

Under the stress and strain of this battle Private Speakman's outstanding powers of leadership were revealed and he so dominated the situation, that he inspired his comrades to stand firm and fight the enemy to a standstill. His great gallantry and utter contempt for his own personal safety were an inspiration to all his comrades. He was, by his heroic actions, personally responsible for causing numerous losses to the enemy, assisting his Company to maintain their position for some four hours and saving the lives of many of his comrades when they were forced to withdraw from their position.

Private Speakman's heroism under intense fire throughout the operation and when painfully wounded was beyond praise and is deserving of supreme recognition.

Certified as a true copy of an Extract from the London Gazette dated 28th December, 1951.

Secretary
Central Chancery of the Orders of Knighthood
St. James's Palace
London SW1

Bill Speakman, VC. The citation for the award of his Victoria Cross.

Above: *Bill Speakman's medals on his Royal Hospital Chelsea tunic.*

Left: *Bill Speakman's Chelsea Pensioners tunic and medals, hanging in his room at the Royal Hospital.*

WILLIAM SPEAKMAN VC
U.K.

Private with the
Black Watch (The Royal Highland Regt) and
The King's Own Scottish Borderers

Served in Korea between
04/07/1951 and 12/08/1952

Born 21/09/1927
Died 20/06/2018

Above: *Bill Speakman's grave memorial is situated at the United Nations Memorial Cemetery, Busan, South Korea.*

Right: *Hill 235, 'Gloster Hill' Gyeonggi-do Province, South Korea.*

Victoria Cross.

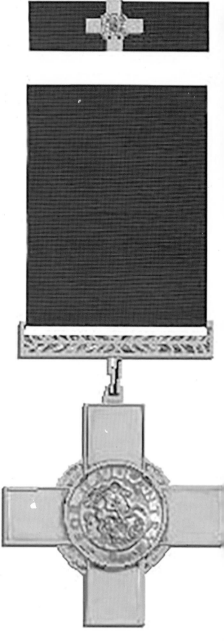

George Cross.

Disabled Centurion tank at Imjin, South Korea.

Yongju, October 1950. British, Australian and American officers in deep discussion.

Flag of South Korea.

British soldiers in South Korea.

Above: *Men of the King's Own Scottish Borderers in the thick of the fighting.*

Right: *British soldier holding a Bren gun in Korea. Notice the cans of beer behind him.*

Above: *Two British soldiers on patrol in Korea.*

Left: *Soldiers of the 1st Battalion, Black Watch, relaxing after the Battle of the Hook 1953.*

Above: *Men of 41st Independent Commando unit laying demolition charges.*

Right: *Derek Kinne was awarded the George Cross for his conduct as a prisoner of war during the Korean War.*

Left: *Lieutenants Terrence Edwaed Waters, GC, on the left and Philip Kenneth Edward Curtis, VC, on the right, both served with the Gloucester Regiment in the Korean War.*

Below: *British soldiers carrying a wounded colleague to safety.*

Right: *Royal Marine on board a ship on his way to Korea.*

Below: *Two members of the Parachute Regiment standing a post in Korea.*

Two British soldiers with a Bren gun, keeping an eye out for the enemy,

Members of the Northumberland Fusiliers in the area of the Imjin River.

Lance Corporal Ward. Also wounded, this non-commissioned officer, by his own personal bravery and steadiness under fire, greatly helped in rallying the men of his platoon. He suffered severe and multiple wounds, necessitation the amputation of his left arm. Lance Corporal Ward displayed exceptional valour, superb courage and tenacious fighting ability.

Sergeant O'Sullivan. During the almost continuous close range fighting throughout the day, he displayed courageous and exemplary conduct, despite his wounds, which was an inspiration to his men.

Private Watts. He fought conspicuously and continuously throughout the day, until he was wounded. The citation speaks of his inspirational bravery, superb fighting qualities and sustained courage.

There was also confirmation from the United Nations command that British forces on the ground at Songju had been wounded and killed by American aircraft who had accidentally dropped bombs at the wrong location. The man who confirmed this was Air Vice – Marshal C.A. Bouchier, the British liaison officer at General MacArthur's headquarters in Tokyo. He explained how five British soldiers had been killed in the unfortunate air strike, as well as a further twenty-five who were wounded.

As the American aircraft took part in three separate engagements on 23 September, it was nigh on impossible to establish in which action the men were killed or wounded. The overall United Nations official casualty returns for the same day record that two officers and thirteen men from other ranks were killed; while four officers and seventy-five men from other ranks were wounded. A further four men were also shown as being missing in action.

It has been estimated that on 23 September 1950, ninety-three members of the Argyll and Sutherland Highlanders became casualties, seventeen of whom were killed, as a result of the 'friendly fire' incident involving the unfortunate error that was made by the American aircraft.

On 6 September 1950, Private Reginald Streeter, of the Middlesex Regiment, and who in civilian life was a plumber's mate from Guildford, Surrey, was shot and killed while on a patrol with his comrades from 1st Battalion, Middlesex Regiment. He was the first British soldier killed during the Korean war. That same day, the Argyll and Sutherland Highlanders experienced their first losses of the war, when Captain Neil Buchannan and his batman, Private Tam Taylor, were also killed. If the realisation that things were now for real hadn't already sunk in for the men of the two regiments, the losses which they sustained on that fateful day made it abundantly clear that their patrols were not a game or some kind of exercise, but real live missions where, sadly, some of them were marked for death.

For the men of the Argyll and Sutherland Highlanders, the death of their two colleagues, didn't subdue them in any way, it simply made them angry. All they wanted was the opportunity to take revenge and even the score. They wouldn't have to wait too long for such an opportunity.

Two weeks later, while returning from a night-time patrol, members of 1st Platoon, 'A' Company, 1st Battalion, Argyll and Sutherland Highlanders, came into contact with a group of North Korean soldiers. The resultant fire fight saw ten of the North Koreans killed. Intentionally or otherwise, the deaths of Captain Buchannan and Private Taylor had been revenged.

On Saturday 20 October 1951, the Argyll and Sutherland Highlanders' annual dinner took place at the St Enoch Hotel in Glasgow. The Regiment's Colonel in Chief, Princess Elizabeth, later Queen Elizabeth ll, sent a 'cable' from Canada, expressing her good wishes:

> Please thank the officers of the Argyll and Sutherland Highlanders holding their annual re-union dinner in St Enoch's Hotel this evening for their kind message of greeting. I hope the distinguished guests dining tonight, may spend a very enjoyable evening.

Four of the Regiment's living holders of the Victoria Cross were present at the function: Colonel Sir Reginald Graham, who won his award for actions at Istabulat, Mesopotamia, on 22 April 1917; Brigadier Lorne M. Campbell, for his actions at Wadi Akarit in Africa on 6 April 1943; Major W.D. Bissett, for his actions at Maine, France on 25 October 1918;

and Captain D.L. Macintyre, for his actions between 24 and 27 August 1918, at Henin, France.

The memory of two other winners of the Victoria Cross, Major K.T. Anderson, who was awarded his posthumous Victoria Cross for his actions at Longstop Hill, in Africa, on 23 April 1943, and Major Kenneth Muir was observed with a minute's silence. The evening included a programme of pipe music by Corporal Skilling from Stirling Castle, including the march, 'Major Kenneth Muir, VC.'

An interesting fact which, having met and interviewed a man who was awarded the Victoria Cross, I feel qualified to add to the discussion is, if you were to meet these men in the street, you wouldn't know them from Adam; they would appear as normal as you and I because they are modesty personified. They do not need, seek or require the platitudes or approval of their peers and others to feel good about themselves.

Their acts of bravery are not for self-effacing reasons, but out of a duty, desire and a singular determination to save the lives of their comrades, no matter what the risk or danger might be to themselves.

Chapter Seven

Lieutenant Terence Edward Waters, GC

Terence Edward Waters was born on the 1st June 1929 in Salisbury, Wiltshire, the elder son of Albert Edward and Muriel Olive Waters. His father, who attended Bristol Grammar School, was a keen sportsman and played sixteen first-class matches for Gloucestershire County Cricket Club between 1923 and 1925.

Terence, and later his younger brother Anthony, also attended Bristol Grammar School between 1940–47, but instead of cricket he excelled at hockey, playing regularly for the school's First XI. He was also part of the school's Cadet Force where he held the rank of sergeant.

On leaving school, Terence applied for and was accepted to attend the Royal Military Academy, Sandhurst, in December 1948, where he was allocated to Ypres Company. Having successfully completed his basic training, he received his commission into the West Yorkshire Regiment as a Second Lieutenant (403718) while in Austria, before volunteering to be sent out to Korea. His application was accepted, and he went out with the Royal Northumberland Fusiliers Regiment (The Prince of Wales Own), before later becoming attached to the 1st Battalion, Gloucestershire Regiment.

The Gloucestershire Regiment had been defending what had officially been designated as Hill 235, near Solma-Li. On the morning of 25 April 1951, the decision was taken by the commanding officer of the 1st Battalion, Gloucestershire Regiment that there was no other option but to pull out from their position and make their way back to the safety of United Nations lines.

A total of 522 officers and soldiers of the Gloucestershire Regiment were captured and became prisoners of war, this included Terence Waters. He was one of the 180 wounded. A total of fifty-nine members of the Regiment were killed in action and of those taken as prisoners of war, thirty-four of them died while being held in captivity.

For their efforts during the Battle of Imjin River, members of the 1st Battalion, Gloucester Regiment, received a total of seven medals. This included two awards of the Victoria Cross, one of which was posthumous, the United States Army's Distinguished Service Cross, two Distinguished Service Orders, the Military Cross twice. They also received the United States Presidential Unit Citation, by order of President Harry S Truman.

The following is an article that was taken from the *London Gazette* newspaper of 13 April 1954. It begins with the following introduction about giving of the award:

> The Queen has been graciously pleased to approve the undermentioned award of the GEORGE CROSS, in recognition of gallant and distinguished service while a prisoner of war in Korea.

The article about Lieutenant Waters actions and what he did to be awarded the George Cross, then followed in a separate article, but in the same edition of the newspaper.

> Lieutenant Waters was captured subsequent to the Battle of the Imjin River, 22nd–25th April 1951. By this time he had sustained a serious wound in the top of the head and yet another most painful wound in the arm as a result of this action.
>
> On the journey to Pyongyang with other captives, he set a magnificent example of courage and fortitude in remaining with wounded other ranks on the march, whom he felt it his duty to care for to the best of his ability.
>
> Subsequently, after a journey of immense hardship and privation, the party arrived at an area west of Pyongyang adjacent to P.W. Camp 12 and known generally as 'The Caves' in which they were held captive. They found themselves imprisoned in a

tunnel driven into the side of a hill through which a stream of water flowed continuously, flooding a great deal of the floor in which were packed a great number of South Korean and European prisoners-of-war in rags, filthy, crawling with lice. In this cavern a number died daily from wounds, sickness or merely malnutrition: they fed on two small meals of boiled maize daily. Of medical attention there was none.

Lieutenant Waters appreciated that few, if any, of his numbers would survive these conditions, in view of their weakness and the absolute lack of attention for their wounds.

After a visit from a North Korean Political Officer, who attempted to persuade them to volunteer to join a prisoner-of-war group known as 'Peace Fighters' (that is, active participants in the propaganda movement against their own side) with a promise of better food, of medical treatment and other amenities as a reward for such activity, an offer that was refused unanimously, he decided to order his men to pretend to accede to the offer in an effort to save their lives. This he did, giving the necessary instructions to the senior other rank with the party, Sergeant Hoper, that the men would go upon his order without fail.

While realising that this act would save the lives of his party, he refused to go himself, aware that the task of maintaining British prestige was vested in him.

Realising that they had failed to subvert an officer with the British party, the North Koreans now made a series of concerted efforts to persuade Lieutenant Waters to save himself by joining the camp. This he steadfastly refused to do. He died a short time after.

He was a young, inexperienced officer, comparatively recently commissioned from the Royal Military Academy, Sandhurst, yet he set an example of the highest gallantry.

Sadly, Lieutenant Terence Edward Waters has no known grave.

For such a young man, he was still only 21 years of age, and regardless of his rank, he was a remarkable individual. The fortitude, concern and empathy which he displayed for, and towards, the men under his command, would usually only be associated with a much older and more experienced soldier than he. He physically helped and cared for his men on their long march to custody, turning down the opportunity of a less arduous journey, as was afforded to officers.

One of those from the 1st Battalion, Gloucestershire Regiment who was also captured and taken as a prisoner of war, was Captain Anthony Farrar-Hockley, who later went on to be General Sir Anthony Farrar-Hockley, Commander in Chief of Allied Forces, Northern Europe in NATO. As the latter he wrote a book that was first published in 1954 entitled *The Edge of the Sword*, which included the following account of the conditions in which he and his fellow Gloucesters were held. He also talks about Terence Waters.

Part of the unworked coal mining settlement of Kangdong, known formerly by prisoners as 'The Caves'. In 1950 and until the summer of 1951, many United Nations prisoners had been crowded into old tunnels in the hillsides round about, often drenched by the water that ran in from underground streams. The numbers of men who died in these black holes in the ground will never be known exactly. In cross checking to find our friends, we accounted for over two hundred and fifty deaths; but this is not the total figure.

How horrible a thought is that? Men having died during their captivity, in an enemy prisoner of war camp, but their names were lost to history and the best that could be afforded them was a name on a memorial. For their loved ones a life time of never knowing where their final resting place was, but simply knowing that they died somewhere in South Korea.

Of all the many stories of gallantry and selfishness on the part of prisoners in these caves, I will recount only one here. A story that was told to us later by men who had formed part of it; a story which provided us with inspiration to continue resistance to our captors during the most difficult moments. Terry, the last remaining platoon commander of 'A' Company, was taken to 'The Caves' in the summer of 1951. He had been a member of a column of seriously wounded captives which marched slowly north from the Imjin River some little time after the two main columns had set off. Though he was in great pain from a wound in his leg and a terrible head injury, Terry set a splendid example on the march, caring, as best he could, for other serious casualties with him. By the time they reached 'The Caves', the condition of many of the prisoners had deteriorated dangerously; for they had had no medical attention of any sort en route and many still wore the dressings, by now ragged and filthy, placed on their wounds by our own medical staff before capture.

That description paints a harrowing picture of the journey these men had to endure. What would have been a difficult enough journey for an able-bodied soldier, must have been a living nightmare for those who were wounded. It could only have been made even worse by the total lack of medical attention and care over the course of a journey that was more than 400 miles in distance.

Terry, and Sergeant Hoper of the Machine Gun Platoon, were placed with a number of others from the column in a cave already crowded with Koreans, themselves dying of starvation and disease. Except when their two daily meals of boiled maize were handed through the opening, they sat in almost total darkness. A subterranean stream ran through the cave to add to their discomfort, and, in these conditions, it was often difficult to distinguish the dead from the dying.

One day a North Korean colonel visited them to put forward a proposition.

'We realise,' he said, 'that your conditions here are uncomfortable. We sympathise. I myself am powerless to help you, unless you are prepared to help us. If you care to join the Peace Movement to fight American Aggression in Korea, we can take you to a proper camp where, in addition to better rations and improved accommodation, your wounds will be cared for by a surgeon.'

Our men refused this offer individually. But Terry, seeing their condition, their numbers dwindling, came to a decision on which he acted the next morning. He drew Sergeant Hoper to one side and said:

'I have thought this business over and have decided that you must go over to the Peace Fighters Camp. Most of you will die if you stay here. Go over, do as little as you can; and remember always that you are British soldiers.'

'What about you sir?' asked Hoper.

'It is different for me,' said Terry. 'I am an officer; I cannot go. But I order you to go and take our men with you.'

Terry remained firm in his decision and when the North Korean colonel returned, as they had guessed he would, Sergeant Hoper and his party left 'The Caves' with a group of American soldiers. The colonel pressed Terry to accompany them, advising him that he would not accept a final decision just then, but would return later.

He returned four times. Armed with promises of an operation on Terry's wounds by a surgeon, and a special diet of eggs, milk and meat in place of the boiled maize, he failed each time.

Terry was a young subaltern, not long out of the Royal Military Academy, Sandhurst. Yet, irrespective of his service and youth, he saw clearly, as an officer representing the British Commonwealth in enemy country, by his actions the Commonwealth's reputation would be judged. Quite simply he was given a choice: life, and agreement to reject, at least outwardly, the principles for which he was fighting in Korea; or a steadfast adherence to those principles, and death. Coolly, loyally, like the gallant officer he was, Terry chose death. And so he died.

What is truly remarkable about this story, is the fact that Terence Waters, was only 21 years of age at the time of his death, despite conducting himself in a manner that would suggest he was much older. His actions showed unbelievable humility. He had the power to determine his own destiny but because he was a proud, principled and virtuous individual, he took care of his men by securing their safety, before acting as a true officer and gentleman and not succumbing to the enticements and bribery laid before him by the enemy in an attempt to make him demean an allied nation and to dishonour his King and Country. None of which he was prepared to do.

Lieutenant 463718 Terence Edward Waters was posthumously awarded the George Cross for his actions while being held as a prisoner of war having been wounded in action and captured by troops of the Chinese People's Volunteer Army. His parents travelled to Buckingham Palace to receive their son's award from Queen Elizabeth II on 6 July 1954. His medals, including his George Cross, Korea Medal with Mentioned in Despatches oakleaf, which is dated 8 December 1953, and United Nations Medal, are kept and displayed at the Soldiers of Gloucestershire Museum, Gloucester. Terence Waters is commemorated at the United Nations Memorial Cemetery at Busan, South Korea, and on war memorials in Stoke Bishop, where he regularly attended church and at Westbury-on-Trym, near Bristol.

Terence's brother, Anthony, also decided on a life in the military and, having completed his National Service, he was in the draft to be sent to Korea; he was due to be deployed in June 1951 but his name was withdrawn, it is believed this occurred largely because of what happened to Terence. Maybe the authorities, knowing that the Waters had already lost one son, didn't want to risk the family possibly losing a second son in the same conflict.

According to British government reports, the Gloucestershire Regiment suffered 620 casualties. This resulted in the Regiment only being able to muster 217 men by the morning of 27 April. A total of 522 members of the Gloucestershire Regiment became prisoners of war, of those 180 were wounded and a further thirty-four died while in captivity. A further fifty-nine members of the Regiment were killed in action during the Battle of Imjin River.

To put some 'meat on the bones' of this story and make it more personal, I have included the details of, and some information about, four of the men who followed Lieutenant Terence Waters into captivity, and whose lives he helped save by getting them out of 'The Caves'. All of the men were from Gloucester, which made their story even more poignant. They were all initially reported as being missing in action, meaning that the uncertainty for their families as to whether they were alive or dead must have been unbearable.

Private Ronald Horsfall, who was 27 years of age, had served during the Second World War with the Northamptonshire Regiment in North Africa, before then fighting his way through Italy, where he took part in the Battle for Monte Cassino. From there he went on to Austria, not returning home to the United Kingdom until 1948. On his return, he remained in the army before being finally discharged in 1949, and placed on the Army Reserve. With the need to send troops to Korea, he was recalled and transferred to the Gloucestershire Regiment and sailed for Korea in 1950. He was one of those captured by the Chinese at the Battle of Imjin River. He was a married man with a 3-year-old daughter.

Private Leonard Allison Jones was another veteran of the Second World War, having enlisted in the army at the outbreak of the war in 1939, he went on to take part in the D-Day Landings, and had been wounded twice by the end of the war. Thankfully, they must have been of a minor nature because on his return to the United Kingdom he was also placed on the Army Reserve and was recalled to active service in August 1950, sailing out to Korea with the Gloucestershire Regiment. He was another of those captured by the Chinese at the Battle of Imjin River.

He was a married man with two children. Yet another family who had to wait to discover if their loved one was alive or dead, and who would have no doubt have been very grateful for Lieutenant Terence Waters' actions.

Private Cecil Roy Williams was not a veteran of the Second World War. In 1951, he was only 20 years of age and a single man who still lived with his parents at 3 Graham Road, Gosport, where he was born. He joined the army when he was only 18 years of age, serving with the 1st Battalion, Dorset Regiment in Austria, and later went to Hong Kong with the 1st Battalion, Wiltshire Regiment. He was later transferred to the Gloucestershire Regiment, and had only arrived in Korea in March 1951, when he was reported as missing in action.

As a boy, Williams was a member of the Christ Church Portsdown Scout Troop. He was also a keen sportsman, representing his school, Canford Cliff in Bournemouth, at rowing and rugby. With his leadership skills already having being recognised, he captained both teams. He was also a sergeant in the school's Junior Training Corps.

In his youth he attended his local schools where he particularly excelled at sport, representing Gosport schools in football against Portsmouth schools at Fratton Park, playing in goal. After leaving school he started working for a local grocer's, before then going on to work for the gas company, and when he turned 18, he chose the army for his National Service.

David John English was 20 years of age and the only son of Lieutenant Commander E.A.V. English, Royal Navy, retired, and Mrs English, of 100 The Brow, Widley. Like Private Williams he was undertaking his National Service, but rather than following in his father's footsteps, and joining the navy, he also chose the army. In June 1950, he received a temporary commission, but fully intended seeking a permanent one after he had completed his National Service.

With the United Kingdom eventually agreeing to send troops to support the United Nations mission, English left for Korea on 2 October 1950, as a Second Lieutenant with the Hampshire Regiment, but was then attached to the 1st Battalion, Gloucestershire Regiment.

A large part of why these men survived the war and made it back home to England is because of Terence Waters' actions in 'The Caves'.

Chapter Eight

Fusilier Derek Godfrey Kinne, GC

Derek Godfrey Kinne, was born in Nottingham on 11 January 1931. His brother Raymond was killed while on active service in Korea while serving with the Argyll and Sutherland Highlanders. It was Raymond's death that spurred him on to enlist in the army and get himself out to Korea. The brothers had made a pact with each other that if something happened to one of them, then the other one would avenge the other's death. What that actually meant for Derek isn't entirely clear, but I have no doubt that it involved killing as many of the enemy as he possibly could.

Derek Kinne enlisted in the army in 1950 and was allocated to the 1st Battalion, Royal Northumberland Fusiliers, serving with them in Korea, where they were part of the United Nations 29th Infantry Brigade under the command of Brigadier Tom Brodie. On 22 April 1951, the brigade was tasked with defending a twelve-mile stretch in the north-west of South Korea, just below the 38th parallel, and right next to the Imjin River. The 1st Battalion, Gloucestershire Regiment, were holding the left flank of the line, with the 1st Battalion, Royal Northumberland Fusiliers, to their right, and the Belgian battalion who were to the right of them on Hill 194.

The battle began on the evening of 22 April when, at just after 2200 hours, elements of the Chinese People's Volunteer Army managed to circumnavigate their way around Belgian forces, which were the only United Nations unit located on the northern side of the Imjin River. The problem with this was that if the Chinese forces could get to the two bridges, they would be able to prevent the Belgians retreating to the comparative safety of the rest of the division. Recognising this as a possibility, Brigadier Brodie sent forward his reserve unit, 1st Battalion, Royal Ulster Rifles, to secure both of the bridges. But no sooner had they reached the bridges than they were engaged by the Chinese forces, some of whom had already began crossing the river.

Kinne was captured at the Battle of Imjin River and spent the next two years in a number of prisoner of war camps. His initial incarceration only came about after a 400-mile enforced march, a journey which took more than a month to complete. But for him, life as a prisoner was never going to be about sitting back and waiting for the war to end. He decided right at the beginning that he was going to try his best to escape and to be a thorn in the backside of his captors. The Chinese guards of one of the camps at which he was held decided they would try to get him to inform on his colleagues; they failed miserably because Kinne was having none of it. His refusal to cooperate with his captors brought him a beating; his response was to hit back at one of the guards, which brought him another beating.

The treatment he received and endured at the hands of his guards would have broken most people, but Kinne was made of stronger stuff, and if all else failed he always had the pact he'd made with his brother to keep him going. Here was a man who volunteered to join the army and volunteered to serve in Korea. He was a man on a mission, and that mission was revenge against the very people who had been responsible for the death of his beloved brother. Wow.

On one occasion a Chinese guard decided to beat him with the butt of his machine gun. Unfortunately for the guard, the gun went off and killed him. What happened next? Yes, you guessed it, Kinne was beaten up by the other guards. He was then placed in solitary confinement, which wasn't in the relative comfort of a cell, but a metal box in the ground. Soon after being released from his below-ground incarceration, he was put on trial for 'attempting to escape and for being a reactionary'. Not surprisingly, he was found guilty, sentenced to twelve months solitary confinement, and asked if he had anything to say. The Chinese obviously did not appreciate his response as they upped his sentence to eighteen months.

One of the funniest things he did while he was a prisoner of war was to agree to write a confession about the camp's supposed escape committee and his part in it. He only agreed to do this if he could have a cigarette to smoke, so one of the guards handed over a lit cigarette, but Kinne asked for the guard's entire pack, saying that it would help him write his confession. After he had completed nearly fourteen pages, one of the guards came and collected what Kinne had written so that it could be translated. The confession began with the heading, 'Goldilocks and the Three Bears.' Once they understood what he had been writing they were furious and beat him up.

Derek Kinne would have been an inspiration to his fellow British prisoners of war, with both his actions and words, along with his unwillingness to submit to his captors' will. He would have definitely helped raise their morale.

He was the man Winston Churchill referred to as 'my British bulldog', for being the prisoner the Chinese could not break.

The Citation for the award of Fusilier Kinne's George Cross, was published in the *London Gazette* on 9 April 1954. It is one of the longest citations for the award of any medal I have ever read.

22105517 Fusilier Derek Godfrey Kinne, the Royal Northumberland Fusiliers.

In August, 1950, Fusilier Kinne volunteered for service in Korea. He joined the 1st Battalion, the Royal Northumberland Fusiliers, and was captured by Chinese Communist forces on 25 April, 1951, the last day of the Imjin River battle. From then on he had only two objects in mind: firstly to escape, and secondly by his contempt for his captors and their behaviour, and his utter disregard for the treatment meted out to him, to raise the morale of his fellow prisoners. The treatment which he received during his period of captivity is summarised in the succeeding paragraphs.

Fusilier Kinne escaped for the first time within 24 hours of capture but was retaken a few days later while attempting to regain our own lines. Eventually he re-joined a large group of prisoners being marched North to prison camps, and despite the hardships of this march, which lasted a month, rapidly emerged as a man of outstanding leadership and very high morale. His conduct was a fine example to all his fellow prisoners.

In July, 1952, Fusilier Kinne, who was by now well known to his captors, was accused by them of being non-cooperative and was brutally interrogated about the other P.W. who had uncooperative views. As a result of his refusal to inform on his comrades, and for striking back at a Chinese officer who assaulted him, he was twice severely beaten up and tied up for periods of twelve and twenty-four hours, being made to stand on tip-toe with a running noose round his neck which would throttle him if he attempted to relax in any way.

He escaped on 27 July but was recaptured two days later. He was again beaten up very severely, and placed in handcuffs (which could be, and frequently were, tightened so as to restrict circulation), from which he was not released until 16 October, 1952, a period of eighty-one days.

He was accused of insincerity, a hostile attitude towards the Chinese, sabotage of compulsory political study, escape, and of being reactionary. From 15 to 20 August he was confined in a very small box cell, where he was made to sit to attention all day, being periodically beaten, prodded with bayonets, kicked and spat upon by the guards, and denied any washing facilities.

On 20 August, 1952, he was made to stand to attention for seven hours and when he complained was beaten by the Chinese guard commander with the butt of a submachine gun, which eventually went off and killed the guard commander. For this Fusilier Kinne was beaten senseless with belts and bayonets, stripped of his clothes, and thrown into a dank rat-infested hole until 19 September. He was frequently taken out and beaten, including once (on 16 September) with pieces of planking until he was unconscious.

On 16 October Fusilier Kinne was tried by a Chinese military court for escape and for being a reactionary and hostile to the Chinese, and was sentenced to twelve months' solitary confinement. This was increased to eighteen months when he complained at his trial of denial of medical attention, including that for a severe double hernia which he had sustained in June, 1952, while training to escape.

On 5 December, 1952, he was transferred to a special penal company. His last award of solitary confinement was on 2 June, 1953, when he was sentenced for defying Chinese orders and wearing a rosette in celebration of Coronation Day.

He was eventually exchanged at Panmunjon on 10 August, 1953. As late as 8 and 9 August he was threatened with non-repatriation for demanding an interview with the International Red Cross Representatives who were visiting Prisoner of War camps.

Fusilier Kinne was, during the course of his periods of solitary confinement, kept in no less than seven different places of imprisonment, including a security police gaol, under conditions of the most extreme degradation and increasing brutality. Every possible method both physical and mental was employed by his captors to break his spirit, a task which proved utterly beyond their powers. Latterly he must have been fully aware that every time he flaunted his captors and showed openly his detestation of themselves and their methods he was risking his life. He was in fact several times threatened with death or non-repatriation. Nevertheless he was always determined to show that he was prepared neither to be intimidated nor cowed by brutal treatment at the hands of a barbarous enemy. His powers of resistance and his determination to oppose and fight the enemy to the maximum were beyond praise. His example was an inspiration to all ranks who came into contact with him.

Lieutenant 407730 Leo Samuel Adams-Acton, who was attached to American Special Forces, and like Fusilier Kinne, was one of those captured at the end of the Battle. Initially he was officially reported as missing in action, presumed dead, but had actually been captured by the Chinese and taken as a prisoner of war. He was then kept in captivity for more than two years in a North Korean prisoner of war camp. On 16 July 1953, he was either shot and killed while trying to escape, or captured in the process of escaping and executed afterwards for his actions. He was a holder of the Military Cross, and at the time of his death was only 23 years of age. His death illustrates just how fortunate Derek Kinne was not to have met a similar fate.

The Royal Northumberland Fusiliers lost a number of officers and men at the Battle of Imjin River.

Fusilier 22299115 Peter Angus was another involved in the Battle of Imjin River, and although he was initially reported as being missing in action, it was later confirmed that he had been killed in action on 23 April 1951.

Fusilier 22331783 Thomas Edward Bloore (but originally Bloor) of, Newcastle was only 19 years of age when he was killed in action on the final day of the battle, 25 April 1951.

Fusilier 22539087 Spencer Dan Broadway, a 23-year-old from Lichfield in Staffordshire was killed in action.

Fusilier 5500178 Basil Leslie Cox, a 30-year-old who hailed from Alresford, Hampshire, was killed in action on 25 April 1951, the last day of the battle.

Fusilier 4271177 Frederick Arthur Curry, who was 33 years of age and a Geordie from Newcastle-Upon-Tyne, was killed in action on 23 April 1951.

Sergeant 21013197 Robert Andrew Donald was 25 years of age from Chelsea in West London. He was killed in action on 24 April 1951.

Fusilier 4272098 Alfred Eke was 34 years of age from Wallsend on Merseyside, when he was killed in action on 23 April 1951.

Fusilier 21036239 Raymond Gordon Ford was 21 years of age when he was killed in action on 25 April 1951. He was from Portobello in Staffordshire.

Fusilier 19031259 Kenneth Foster was 22 years of age and from Huddersfield in Yorkshire. He was killed in action on 23 April 1951.

Lieutenant Colonel Kingsley Osbern Nugent Foster, DSO, OBE, was 44 years of age when he was killed in action on 25 April 1951. He was from Redhill in Surrey. He had joined the Regiment in 1925, and went on to serve with them in China and India. At the outbreak of the Second World War he went out to North Africa with the Eighth Army, and in 1944, he was given command of the 7th Battalion, Manchester Regiment which was involved with the liberation of Holland.

A career soldier he returned to England after the war, where he remained for two years, before being temporarily promoted to the rank of Colonel, and posted to Singapore and Malaya. In 1950 he turned down a promotion to the rank of brigadier and a posting to India, as well as relinquishing his position and rank in Singapore, to return to the rank of lieutenant colonel, in order to command the Royal Northumberland Fusiliers, which was then sent out to Korea.

Lance Corporal 4615187 Harry Hamer was 31 years of age from Elland, Halifax. He was killed in action on 23 April 1951.

Lance Corporal 5123706 J Kain was 29 years of age when he was killed in action on the last day of the battle, 25 April 1951. He was from Birmingham.

Fusilier 14474759 Derrick Langley, from Middlesbrough, was 23 years of age when he was killed in action on 25 April 1951.

Fusilier 3189424 John McDonald, from Dumfries in Scotland was 29 years of age. He was killed in action on 23 April 1951.

Lance Corporal 21072543 D Oldfield, from Halifax in West Yorkshire was 21 years of age. He was killed in action on 23 April 1951.

Fusilier 22348750 Clive Sadler was from Middlesbrough and was 19 years of age. He was killed in action on 25 April 1951. He was one of the Regiment's eleven young men of that age who were killed during the war.

Fusilier 5949689 Thomas Sharp, from Southwark, London was 29 years of age. He was killed in action on 25 April 1951.

Fusilier 22331471 Raymond Sugden was 19 years of age and from Hull. He died of his wounds on 26 April 1951.

Fusilier 22540096 Derek Edward Tamblyn was from Birmingham, and was 23 years of age at the time of his death on 25 April 1951.

Fusilier 22314975 James Taylor, who was from Ashington in Northumberland, was 20 years of age when he was killed in action on 25 April 1951.

Lance Corporal 22314976 Gerald Albert Thornton was 19 years of age from Newcastle-Upon-Tyne. He was killed in action on 25 April 1951.

Fusilier 22267850 Lawrence Walker was from Bradford and 23 years of age. He was killed in action on 25 April 1951.

Fusilier 22538099 Thomas Walne was from Burnley and 25 years of age when he was killed in action on 25 April 1951.

Fusilier 1429896 William Charles Wellman was 30 years of age from Poole in Dorset. He was killed in action on 25 April 1951.

Fusilier 22328907 Keith Wintersgill, from Earby, Skipton, Yorkshire was 19 years of age when he was killed in action on 25 April 1951.

Fusilier 22185644 Ronald Winterton, from Dormanstown, Yorkshire, was also 19 years of age when he died of his wounds on 28 April 1951.

Seven of the above men have no known grave as their bodies were never discovered, but their names are recorded on the United Nations Wall of Remembrance, which can be found within the confines of the United

Nations Memorial Cemetery in the City of Busan, South Korea, where the rest of the above named men are buried.

All of these men were comrades of Fusilier Derek Kinne, many of whom he would have no doubt seen killed before he and other members of the battalion were captured, and marched off to captivity on 25 April 1951.

Chapter Nine

Korean war through the eyes of the press

The Belfast News Letter, dated Friday 21 July 1950, included the following article about the Korean war, and Russia's attitude in particular:

> The Russian attitude to the Korean war, as stated by Mr Gromyko to the British Ambassador in Moscow, is exceedingly cynical. Russia's desire to have Communist China appointed to the Security Council is understandable, but it is hard to believe that she considers the issue worth the risk of a third world war. Yet she courts that risk if she attaches the Chinese condition to the ending of the Korean aggression. Members of the Security Council are not of one mind on this matter, nor were they before the Korean attack. The United Kingdom has not voted for admission of the Chinese Communists, but it has not voted against it, and it is believed to have done what it could behind the scenes to influence a favourable vote. It made it known that as soon as six other members were in favour of changing the Chinese representative, it would make the vital seventh vote. The Russians are adept at confusing an issue, and they must be glad of the opportunity to introduce in to the Korean question, on which the free nations are almost wholly at one, the secondary question of Communist China, upon which the free nations are quite sharply divided. Members of the United Nations, whatever their view on that point, would be well advised to give the Korean war first place in their minds and not allow the secondary issue to divide them. The situation does not seem to have been helped by Mr Nehru's excursion into appeasement, but Mr Atlee has made it clear that the British government is not prepared to enter into a bargain

over Korea. His comment on President Truman's message to Congress is in his customary restrained style, but no doubt he means what he says when he announces his Government's intention to 'see what can be done' to match the high purpose and resolve of the President.

How interesting to note that just four days after this political discord, North Korea crossed the 38th parallel and began its invasion of neighbouring South Korea, and within just four days her troops had taken the capital, Seoul. During the year prior to invading South Korea, Kim Il-Sung had personally travelled to Moscow to meet with Stalin, where he asked Russia to provide him with military aid so he could once again reunite Korea as one nation, adding that he felt confident of victory. Stalin refused to aid North Korea, and advised Kim Il-Sung against such action.

It wasn't long before the United Nations forces, who had intervened in support of South Korea and were under the command of General MacArthur, made an impactive intervention, not only by halting the North Koreans' attack, but by forcing them back beyond the divide which separated the two countries.

The 'should we or shouldn't we' issue as to whether American forces should stop once they had forced the North Koreans back beyond the 38th parallel, caused great debate in Washington. There were those in the American State Department who felt that MacArthur should stop once that point had been reached, believing that it was too risky to go any further, while there were others who felt the exact opposite, mainly because they did not see that the 38th parallel was ever intended to be a permanent political boundary between the two halves of the Korean peninsula. The Pentagon, where the United States Department of Defense is situated, agreed with the latter opinion believing that to simply stop just because they had reached the 38th parallel, would result in even more military instability between the two sides. If North Korea had decided to take such action without any warning once, then she could just as easily and readily do it again. The question was: when? In part, it was this uncertainty that resulted in the decision of MacArthur to continue his pursuit of North Korean forces. From a South Korean perspective, they couldn't have been happier, because if MacArthur was ultimately successful it would mean a united Korea and not a Communist one.

For President Truman it was not a straight forward decision to make, and he had to take a lot into consideration before giving his stamp of approval for MacArthur to continue past the 38th Parallel. China as a Communist state had only been in existence since 1948, so to a large extent she was an unknown quantity, but this also made her unpredictable. In such an early stage of existence, and at a time where she sought international recognition, the last thing that she could ill-afford was to appear weak on the world stage.

One of Truman's responses to North Korea's attack on the South had been to move his Seventh Fleet to defend Taiwan should Communist China decide to invade their Chinese Nationalist counterparts there. These political manoeuvrings by the United States caused concern among the Communist Chinese authorities. There were worries that they might be enough of an encouragement to those in China who were anti-Communist to rise up. The deployment of America's Seventh Fleet to Taiwan was seen as a direct attempt to interfere with her internal matters.

Communist China had to show strength, not only on the world political stage, but to her own people, to show them that they were a force to be reckoned with and could not be pushed around.

As for President Truman, he knew that he had to be decisive yet cautious at the same time, because if he made a mistake in the way he dealt with North Korea, there was a big risk that it might bring China, and/or Russia, into the war on the North's side, which ran the risk of igniting a Third World War, just five years after the Second World War had finished.

Whether MacArthur should be allowed to cross the 38th parallel and pursue the North Korean forces was not an easy decision. Truman looked to his advisors both in the State Department and the Central Intelligence

Agency to make clear his options. He was told that China would not attack United States forces in North Korea, that it was no more than a bluff, and because of her delicate economy she could ill-afford to become embroiled in any kind of war, especially when she had so many other matters to deal with.

North Korean leader Kim Il-Sung, realising the perilous situation he found himself in, sent two of his high-ranking officials to Beijing to request China's assistance by sending troops to North Korea. Shortly afterwards China announced that if American forces crossed the 38th parallel, she would intervene on the side of North Korea.

As North Korea was a Russian occupied zone, it would have appeared strange to interested observers if she did not intervene militarily in North Korea. It would appear at the time that China acquiesced to Russia's requests. By 9 October China had already massed her armies along the length of the Yalu River, which marked her border with North Korea. The next day a meeting took place in Moscow which was attended by Chinese and Russian officials, including Stalin. The topic of the conversation was, not surprisingly, the worsening situation in North Korea. At this meeting Russia suggested that China should assist North Korea with troops, as she, Russia, had already signed an agreement with the United States to pull all her troops out of North Korea. America had pulled its troops out of South Korea in June 1949. Russia also reminded China of how the world might view their situation with the United States if she wasn't seen to stand up to them.

But it is quite possible that Russia had another agenda, by which I mean she did not want to risk being dragged into a conflict or war with the United States. The Second World War had been devastating for Russia who, by conservative estimates, had lost in excess of 20,000,000 men, women and children. She had the experience of being invaded and occupied, albeit briefly, by the forces of Nazi Germany, and the financial cost to her economy had been astronomical. As far as Stalin and his government were concerned, this was something they were happy to keep an eye on, from the sidelines, without becoming fully involved.

Russia agreed to provide China with military equipment and ammunition, but added that she wanted payment for what she supplied, which didn't go down too well with the Chinese authorities in Beijing.

The Glorious Gloucesters at the Battle of Imjin River
The Daily Mirror carried a truly amazing article on the back page of its edition dated Wednesday 13 June 1951, under the heading:

> **Glorious Gloucesters may have been Avenged**
> The Glorious Gloucesters who fought heroically against overwhelming odds in the last Communist offensive in Korea, may have been avenged. American troops who met and defeated Chinese units on Monday, believe they were those who overran the Gloucesters.
>
> An American company commander, whose unit killed twenty-two Chinese and captured eleven, said that when the dead and prisoners were searched, most of them carried or wore British equipment, one of them had a Gloucester cap badge.
>
> British field belts, money, wallets and Sten guns were found and some of the captured Chinese wore British socks and carried ground sheets and other equipment taken from British troops.
>
> Private Gallagher from Brooklyn, New York, recovered a British water bottle on which had been scratched the initials 'JD', while another American unstrapped a British Army waist belt from a bedraggled Chinese prisoner.
>
> Sergeant Rosenberg, from New York, stood on a hilltop and grimly surveyed twenty-two sprawling bodies. 'Maybe we did not get them all, but at least we paid part of the bill. My boys are glad they had a part in doing this,' he said.

What The Gloucestershire Regiment did at the Battle of Imjin River has been told and retold many times over the years. It exemplified the best attitude of the British soldier in fighting on against overwhelming odds, and showed the

Gloucestershire Regiment up as the shining light of what the British military establishment was capable of. The battle resulted in two of its members being awarded the Victoria Cross and another being awarded the George Cross. Two more received the Distinguished Service Order, while another two received the Military Cross. Lieutenant-Colonel James Power Carne, and Major Kenneth Muir, both received the American award of the Distinguished Service Cross, whilst the Gloucestershire Regiment's 1st Battalion, received a United States Presidential distinguished unit citation.

Also in *The Daily Mirror,* Tuesday 19 June 1951:

Korea War Latest
29th Brigade to be Relieved
The British 29th Brigade which has been fighting in Korea since November is to be relieved early in the winter, a War Office message to the Brigade HQ in Tokyo said yesterday. It will be replaced by another brigade, which one, has yet to be decided. At least one of the 29th Brigade's battalions is expected to leave Korea by October.

The Brigade, commanded by Brigadier Thomas Brodie, consists of the 1st Battalions of the Northumberland Fusiliers, the Royal Ulster Rifles, as well as the Gloucestershire Regiment.

The Brigade bore the brunt of the big Communist offensive in April and lost more than 1,000 men killed, wounded or missing in action, mostly men of the 'Glorious Gloucesters'.

Allied patrols met only slight resistance from the Chinese on the western front, the 8th Army communique said. But on the central front the Chinese were reported to be moving up reinforcements and supplies in readiness for a new stand.

Six Russian type MIG jet fighters were destroyed and two damaged yesterday in air battles in 'MIG Alley,' over north-western Korea yesterday.

It is interesting to consider what the fighting in Korea could have led to. If North Korean and Chinese forces had caused United Nations forces to either surrender or retreat, physically withdrawing all of its troops from the peninsula in the process, would Korea have reverted to being just one nation, a Communist one? If United Nations forces had won the day, captured all of the North Korean forces and pushed all Chinese forces out of Korea, would the Soviet Union have sent in ground forces to help stave off a total defeat and if so, would that have led to World War Three?

The remarkable story of the corporal who failed to salute a general, was reported in *The Daily Mirror* on Saturday 15 September 1951.

Corporal Roland Allnut of the 1st Battalion, Gloucestershire Regiment, was a survivor of the stand at Imjin River; a soldier who had fought bravely alongside the men who had greatness bestowed upon them by the awards of the Victoria Cross and other such gallantry medals.

Here is his remarkable and somewhat humorous story:

In the plane taking him for a spot of well-earned leave out of the Korean battleline, Corporal Roland Allnut did wonder once or twice why troops of so many different nationalities were on board.

There were Australians, Canadians, Philippinos, Belgians, Turks, Siamese, Frenchmen, Columbians and Dutchmen. But no one had told him what was going to happen to him, and when they did, it knocked the wind out of him.

As he stepped off the transport plane in Tokyo, he walked straight in to the arms of a bevy of attractive women who kissed him, covered him with garlands of flowers and presented him with a rose covered Key to Tokyo.

Roland, who was 24 years of age and from Hampton Hill in Middlesex, was then gathered in by a trio of Generals, one Australian and two Americans.

In the background a smart American Army band played 'Rule Britannia'. The reason for all this pomp and ceremony? Because he was the 100,000th soldier to be flown to Japan under the United

Nations Rest and Recuperation programme, more commonly referred to as 'R and R.'

Then he was informed that all of the soldiers from the different nations who had been on the aircraft with him, were in fact the 'honour guard' specially selected to do him proud.

Waiting to greet him were a number of high-ranking military personnel, including the British commander in chief of British and Commonwealth troops in Japan, Lieutenant Colonel Sir Horace Robertson; United States Major-General Walker Weible; and Brigadier-General John Henebry, United States Air Force.

Although an impressive turn out in military terms, it is most probably true to say that he was more suitably impressed with the twelve very attractive American Red Cross girls who were waiting to cover him in Hawaiian style flower garlands.

He was then handed the 'Key of Tokyo' by Miss Kate Meyricke from New Whitley in Yorkshire, who was a member of the Women's Volunteer Services Overseas branch.

To say that Corporal Allnut was surprised, astonished, and left almost in a state of shock, was an understatement. If that wasn't enough for the poor man, the day of surprises continued when Miss Meyricke leant forward and gave him a kiss on the cheek, and asked, 'Are you married?' Roland replied, 'Yes, and I'll get in to trouble if she sees a picture of this.'

The Dublin Evening Herald carried an article on Monday 29 October 1951 which put war and peace into some kind of perspective:

Home to City of Silence
It was dark and wet as 117 men in uniform went out in to the city's streets last night. They walked along quietly, apparently unnoticed.

They might have been just any squaddies, but they did seem a little hurt, although all they said was, 'The city seems a bit quiet.' The city in question was Gloucester.

The men were some of the Glorious Gloucesters back from Korea, men who had brought the brightest lustre to the name of the city's county regiment.

I heard only one 'welcome home' gesture; a cinema manager gave them free seats for a film show.

The men, all Z reservists of the 1st Battalion, the Gloucestershire Regiment, had travelled overnight from Liverpool after arriving on the troopship, the Devonshire on Saturday.

All day yesterday they filed in to the barracks depot, going through the last stages of being demobbed before going home.

This suggests that many of these men had completed their National Service and were returning to civilian life. Men who were between the ages of 18 and 30 were liable to be called up. Initially this had been for a period of eighteen months, but after the outbreak of the Korean war in 1950, this was increased to two years.

There was sun-tanned Private Joe Renouf, of Wednesbury in Staffordshire, looking forward to seeing his daughter who was born while he fought by the Imjin River. There was 34-year-old Raymond Barrat, going back to his wife, two children and his plasterer's job in Jersey, and farm worker, Private John Mortlock of Clare, Suffolk, and Private William Stonehouse of South Shields.

All of the men, who had won a special United States citation, were given a military character reference not exceeding 'very good.' They have served only a year since their recall and only men with three years' service can qualify for the army's highest military character, exemplary.

An article entitled 'Allies Win Hand to Hand Battle – Radar Raids in Korea – Coastal Shelling', appeared in the *Liverpool Echo* on Friday

16 November 1951, and would have sent shock waves through the hearts of parents, wives, friends and relatives of British soldiers serving in Korea. The piece contained a statement made by a United States Army officer, Lieutenant Colonel James Hanley, about atrocities committed by North Koreans against prisoners of war.

During the Second World War, Colonel Hanley was in command of the 2nd Battalion, 442nd Infantry, during the fierce battles of the Vosges, and also led his Japanese-American Company in the rescue of the 'Lost Battalion' in the mountains of eastern France.

After the end of the Second World War he remained in the army, and during the Korean war he was the chief of the War Crimes Section of the United States 8th Army.

His statement, blunt and to the point, made the claim that Communist forces were murdering Allied prisoners. The United Nations were so concerned with the allegations that they sent a senior officer of the Public Information Service to Korea, the same day that the story appeared in the press.

Despite Lieutenant Colonel Hanley's seniority and military experience, he had been reprimanded for making the revelation, although a command officer of the United States Army later clarified that it was not an official reprimand, adding that any such action would ever only take place after any subsequent investigation.

Colonel Hanley's comments, submitted by him through official channels, in relation to information censorship, somehow managed to slip through the Command's press advisory division situated in Tokyo and was then sent out to numerous news agencies, although strangely enough, this did not include those in Tokyo.

The British Foreign Office were understandably surprised and concerned by the announcement, which specifically mentioned the deaths of ten British soldiers.

In the report, Colonel Hanley, whose office was in Pusan, alleged that the Chinese and North Koreans had killed thousands of Allied prisoners of war captured since the beginning of the war.

Regardless of how accurate the information released by Colonel Hanley was, it was not the kind of information that the United Nations or Allied military authorities would have wanted releasing for general consumption. Such an announcement was bound to have an effect on morale, both among the soldiers fighting the war and their loved ones back home in the United Kingdom. Politically it wasn't good either because the last thing politicians wanted was a loss of public support over the war and pressure being applied to them for answers and demands to get the troops home.

One aspect of the announcement that was surprising was that it had been made without the knowledge of the United Nations command, the Public Information Service in Tokyo, or the Commander of the United States Eighth Army, Lieutenant General Van Fleet.

The claim that Lieutenant General Van Fleet was unaware of the disclosure by Colonel Hanley, was somewhat ironic, as Hanley's report included a claim that his information had been gleaned from lists of atrocities which had been collected by the Eighth Army, with the numbers of those who had been killed having been verified. Hanley informed the news agencies in Pusan that the release of the information had nothing to do with the ceasefire talks, simply that he wanted 'to point out the near barbarism of the Chinese Communist forces'.

Despite official concern and surprise, both politically and militarily, over the release, the information contained in the report was not contested, and there was no attempt to deny or make counter claims in relation to it. Having said that, United Nations Command officers in Tokyo were concerned about the timing of the announcement, especially as it was done without their permission or authority, and at a time when the whole question of prisoners was being considered on the agenda of ceasefire negotiations. The whole ceasefire issue was a somewhat strange affair as the one that took place in November 1951, at Panmunjon, was the twenty-third such meeting, and the war still went on for another eighteen months. The meeting only lasted for just over two hours, but those conducting the negotiations didn't seem to be able to get past where a demarcation line should be. The United Nations delegates informed their Communist counterparts that they wanted all fighting to stop along the line of contact at the signing of the armistice.

In the United States, President Truman commented that if true, the murders would be the most uncivilised thing that had happened in the past century, but admitted that he had received no direct information on the matter. Although Truman's comments were, to an extent, understandable, he had obviously spoken without thinking about what he was saying, because only six years earlier the world had been utterly shocked at the news of the millions of lives lost in the Holocaust been carried out by Nazi Germany.

On Thursday 15 November 1951, nearly all parts of Korea, North and South, were covered in a blanket of rain and fog, making movement dangerous and fighting even more difficult. The United States Eighth Army reported that United Nations forces north-west of Yanggu had held and consolidated positions which they had captured the previous day.

The British destroyer, HMS *Comus*, attacked a large Communist force, which it had discovered on an island that was only forty miles from the Yalu River, on the west coast of Korea, while HMS *Whitesand Bay*, a royal naval frigate, shelled other Communist forces south-west of Chinnampo.

The Australian destroyer, HMAS *Tobruk*, shelled railway lines, targets that were near Tanchon and Songjin, while other United Nations vessels carried out similar attacks elsewhere.

How strange that all of this fighting was going on at the exact same time that leaders from both sides were sitting around a table trying to put a ceasefire in place. It somehow just didn't add up, and certainly did not make sense.

With Christmas of 1951 on the immediate horizon, the article also described how Colonel J.R.H. Hutchison, who was the Financial Secretary to the War Office, informed the House of Commons that the War Minister hoped this year to be able to repeat the scheme under which parcels weighing up to three pounds could be sent post-free by air mail to their loved ones serving in Korea and nearby Malaya. Just as he had raised everybody's hopes, he then said that he could not give 'a definite promise at this stage', but added that the matter was under review, but with the pressure in the Far and Middle East on the increase, it was becoming more difficult. It would have been a much better idea not to have even mentioned the matter until he knew for certain it was definitely going to take place.

The same article also included the news that the 56th casualty list that had been issued by the War Office on Friday 16 November 1951, contained some 228 names, with the heaviest numbers coming from the Royal Leicestershire Regiment and the King's Own Scottish Borderers.

Evidence of the lack of total support for the war was evident, when nine back bench Labour MPs placed a motion before the House of Commons calling on the government to take all reasonable steps to urgently secure an end to the fighting in Korea. The wording of the motion was as follows;

That this House, having regard to the devastating economic consequences to this country and Western Europe and the increased danger of a world war arising, urge the government to declare publicly its belief, and take all reasonable steps urgently to secure that fighting in Korea shall forthwith cease on the basis of the armistice line already agreed.

That China, under her active government should be accorded her rightful place in the United Nations.

That free elections be held under the supervision of the four occupying powers for a central government of all Germany, and that a disarmament conference be called to arrange genuine and progressive disarmament under agreed conditions for international inspection and control.

The *Sunday Mirror* of 2 December 1951, included an article about an advance party of soldiers from the 1st Battalion, Gloucestershire Regiment, who had returned home to the United Kingdom.

The Dockers Cheer 12 Shy Soldiers
Twelve shy soldiers with tiny blue and gold flashes on their shoulders filed off the troopship, the Empire Halladale at Liverpool

yesterday, and dockers, taximen and porters joined a little group of relatives to cheer them.

The advance party of 'The Glorious Gloucesters' were home and reticent about the page of English history they wrote on the Imjin River in Korea.

Major John Watkin Williams, in charge, said: 'We are here to prepare for the homecoming of the 1st Battalion later this month.'

Company Sergeant Major Arthur Courtney, of Colchester, said modestly, 'It was some fight and we're all glad to be back.' He blushed as he explained to a questioning docker that the blue and gold flashes were the US Presidential citation, the highest American battle honour.

Also on the ship were 600 men of the South Staffs and the Royal Ulster Rifles.

The sight of his daughter, aged two-and-a-half, whom he had never seen before, was too much for Corporal George Garrington, of Birmingham.

Ignoring red tape, he sprinted down the gang-plank with a large teddy bear. The other troops cheered and an officer who started to stride angrily towards him stopped and smiled as tiny Lesley, born after George sailed for the far East, asked, 'Are you my Daddy?'

The remainder of the Gloucesters will arrive at Southampton on December 20.

It would have been a bittersweet moment for these men returning to the United Kingdom, some seven months after the Battle of Imjin River. They would have no doubt been thinking of the fifty-nine of their fellow Gloucestershire Regiment members who were killed in action during the battle. The thirty-nine who were wounded in action and removed to safety during the fighting. The 522 who were captured and became prisoners of war, 180 of whom were wounded. Of these, thirty-four would go on to die while in captivity, never to return home to their loved ones.

Chapter Ten

Korean war

It is important to understand that the Korean war took place under the auspices of the United Nations, not the United States of America, who at no time ever declared war on North Korea, China, or even Russia for that matter. As far as the American President, Harry S. Truman was concerned, the nation's involvement was what he described as a 'police action'. By the time the Korean war had come to an end, 36,574 American military personnel had been killed, and more than 100,000 had been wounded, so regardless of the original political intention, it certainly didn't end up as a police action.

As for Great Britain, initially she even declined to send ground troops to serve in Korea, and only changed her mind when the government of the time became concerned about their reputation on the world stage, and of worries about the damage that might be caused to their relationship with the United States, by their reluctance.

In some respects it was a strange affair. Maybe because of its timing, it has often been referred to as the 'Forgotten War', but not because people didn't give a damn, but because it just didn't seem to attract that much of the public's attention, unless of course a family had a loved one fighting in it.

Remember that this was taking place just five years after the end of the Second World War, so we are talking about a time when people had had enough of war, killing and suffering. Because four of the most powerful nations in the world – Russia, China, the United Kingdom and the United States – were involved, there was real concern that the Korean war could end up turning in to a third world war, which was something that no government wanted, nor could they afford.

During the years from the end of the Second World War in 1945 and throughout the 1950s, the United Kingdom was involved in a number of other military conflicts around the world besides Korea.

The Iran crisis of 1946

This crisis came about as a result of the refusal of Stalin's Soviet Union to relinquish occupied Iranian territory, despite a number of promises that it would do so within six months of the end of the Second World War. Soviet forces eventually pulled out of Iran on 15 December 1946.

The Greek Civil War

Between 30 March 1946 and 16 October 1949, Greek forces loyal to the Greek government and supported by those from the United States and the United Kingdom, came into conflict with the Democratic Army of Greece, and military elements from Yugoslavia, Bulgaria, Albania and the Soviet Union.

The Malayan Emergency

Between 16 June 1948 and 12 July 1960, Democratic and Communist forces fought to take control of Malaya. The non-Communist Federation of Malaya, supported by forces from Fiji, South Africa, Australia, New Zealand, United Kingdom, Thailand, Nepal, and Southern Rhodesia, were fighting against the Communist Party of Malaya, the Soviet Union, China, North Vietnam and Indonesia.

Anglo-Egyptian War

Between 1951 and 1952, British forces stationed at the Suez Canal had to endure a sustained campaign from Egyptian guerrillas who were aided in their efforts by the Egyptian government. Britain had sent 60,000 troops to defend the Suez Canal in October 1951, after a rise in Egyptian Nationalism. It was the biggest airlift of British troops since the Second World War. The guerrilla campaign was also carried out against British and Western targets. On 25 January 1952, British forces retaliated by attacking an Egyptian police station. By the end of the attack, fifty Egyptian police officers were dead and another 100 wounded.

Invasion of Hamasa

For three years between 1952 and 1955, a number of attempts were made to influence the loyalties of tribes located in and around the Buraimi Oasis.

Saudi Arabian forces were up against those from the Trucial Oman Scouts, forces of the British Empire and the Sultanate of Muscat and Oman.

The Mau Mau Uprising

Between 1952 and 1960, British forces fought against the Kenya Land and Freedom Army, also known as the Mau Mau. In essence, it was a war between a number of Kenyan tribes who wanted independence from British colonial rule and white European colonist settlers.

Cyprus

Between 1955 and 1959, there was a rebellion by Greek Cypriots who were against British rule.

The Suez Crisis

In 1956 Israeli forces invaded Egypt, followed by French and British forces. The aim of the invasion was to regain Western control of the Suez Canal and remove the Egyptian President, Gamal Abdel Nasser from power, after he nationalised the Canal.

Korea had not been the master of its own destiny for many years. China and Imperial Japan had gone to war with each other over the country, during the First Sino-Japanese War of 1894 and 1895. Japan's victory saw Korea enjoy a ten year period of independence and self-rule, before in 1905, Japan made Korea its protectorate.

A protectorate is a dependent territory which has been granted local autonomy with some independence, while still recognising the ultimate authority of a controlling sovereign state. In exchange for this subservience, the protectorate usually accepts specified obligations, which may differ greatly depending on the true nature of their relationship. In layman's terms, a protectorate is an autonomous area under the overall control of a higher sovereignty.

The Japan-Korea Annexation Treaty of 1910 meant that Korea, in effect, became part of the Imperial Japanese Empire, and in doing so surrendered control of her own internal affairs. This led many Korean nationalists to flee the country, a number of whom made their way to China where, in 1919, they set up what they named the Provincial Government of the Republic of Korea, which sadly failed to acquire any international recognition. Their situation wasn't helped by the fact that from 1919 until the outbreak of the Second World War, any and all defiance of Japan's control over the country was entirely led by the Communist party of Korea.

The People's Liberation Army and the National Revolutionary Army in China helped the Koreans who had taken refuge in their country with their struggle against the Japanese, in a military sense. This wasn't as straightforward as it might sound, as parts of China were also occupied by Japanese forces. As the war unfolded, the Korean Communists took on the Japanese in both Korea, and Manchuria in China. As for the Korean Nationalists, they fought against the Japanese throughout the Burma campaign which continued from 1941 until the end of the Second World War in 1945.

In November 1943, the Cairo Conference took place in Egypt, with the purpose of determining who was going to get what when the war was won. Those in attendance at the meeting were Winston Churchill, Franklin D. Roosevelt, and Chiang Kai-shek, Chairman of the Government of the Republic of China. Joseph Stalin chose not to attend because in 1941 Russia and Japan had signed a five year neutrality agreement, which meant the two nations had agreed not to go to war with each other for a period of five years. If Stalin had attended the meeting, it would not have gone down well with the Japanese, that he had chosen to share centre stage with the other three leaders, as Japan was at war with each of their countries.

The conference lasted for five days between 22 and 26 November 1943 and one of the outcomes was an agreement between China, the United Kingdom and the United States of America, stating that 'in due course Korea shall become free and independent', which was very magnanimous of the three nations to decide the fate of another country, without consulting them.

Before the end of the war, two more similar conferences took place. In November 1943 there was the Tehran conference in Iran, code-named 'Eureka', which was a strategy meeting of what became termed 'The Big Three', Churchill, Roosevelt and Stalin.

It would be fair to say that although the three leaders arrived with differing objectives, the main outcome of the conference was the Western Allies' commitment to open a second front against Nazi Germany. Besides other matters, the conference also addressed the Allies' operations against Imperial Japan, and the envisaged post-war settlement.

Between 4 and 11 February 1945, there was the Yalta conference, code-named Argonaut and Magneto, which once again saw Churchill, Roosevelt and Stalin sit round a table with their advisers to discuss the post-war reorganisation of Germany and Europe.

The main aim of the conference was to shape a lasting post-war peace that represented a collective security order as well as a plan to give self-determination to the liberated peoples of post-Nazi Europe. The meeting was intended mainly to discuss the re-establishment of the nations of war-torn Europe. But with what became known as the 'Cold War', or a state of political tension between Eastern and Western Bloc countries, it is debatable just how successful the conference was.

The Potsdam Conference, held in Potsdam, Germany, took place between 17 July and 2 August 1945. With Roosevelt now dead, the United States of America was represented by President Harry S Truman. Stalin once again represented the Soviet Union, while the United Kingdom had two representatives over the course of the conference. It began with Winston Churchill, who was replaced on 28 July by Clement Atlee, who had defeated Churchill in the British general election. The conference looked at how to administer post-war Germany and established a post-war order, considered peace treaty issues, and how to counter the effects of the war.

There were real similarities between what took place in Korea as a result of the November 1941 Cairo Conference, and the outcome for post-war Germany following the Potsdam Conference; each of the countries were split in two, with a Soviet and Allied zone, which created a protracted military stand-off between Communism and Capitalism.

Despite the neutrality agreement Russia did eventually declare war on Japan – on 9 August 1945, three days after the Americans had dropped an atomic bomb on Hiroshima. The next day, Soviet forces began their occupation of northern Korea, although it is not clear whether Stalin had informed the Allied nations of his intentions.

That same evening in Washington, two American colonels, Dean Rusk and Charles H. Bonesteel lll, were extremely busy devising a plan for how best to divide the Korean peninsula into Russian and American sectors. They came up with the 38th parallel as the location where the country should be divided.

This was part of what was General Order No.1, the document prepared by the United States' Joint Chiefs of Staff and approved by President Truman on 17 August 1945, and formed part of the Japanese surrender at the end of the Second World War.

On 2 September 1945, General Douglas MacArthur delivered General Order No.1 to the staff of the Japanese Imperial General Headquarters. The Order covered numerous elements, including instructions on where, and to whom the Japanese should surrender. It also included the occupation of areas that had previously been under the control of Japanese forces, and informed them of which Allied nation would take over supervision.

In relation to Korea, it outlined how the country would be divided at the 38th parallel, with the instruction that Japanese troops north of that line should surrender to Soviet forces, while those stationed south of the line should surrender to the Commander in Chief, United States Forces in the Pacific, General Douglas MacArthur.

Explaining why he and Colonel Bonesteel lll had chosen the division of the country to be at the 38th Parallel, Colonel Rusk observed, 'even though it was further north than could be realistically reached by US forces, in the event of Soviet disagreement, we felt it important to include the capital of Korea in the area of responsibility of American troops.'

So there you have it, the choice of the 38th parallel, as a dividing line wasn't just a random selection but a strategic one, and possibly more politically motivated than militarily.

There will always be an unknown element to this equation: what would have happened if Stalin had not agreed to the 38th parallel being the dividing line? It also raises another question: why did he agree to it, knowing that it immediately gave the Americans control of the nation's capital? Perhaps because he didn't know the Americans didn't have sufficient resources to be able to fully occupy South Korea, before his own troops could have occupied the entire country. Thankfully, Stalin, who had breached a few of the agreements and pacts he had signed over the years, maintained his wartime approach of cooperation with America and her allies. When his troops reached the 38th Parallel they not only stopped, but they then had to wait a further three weeks before United States forces even arrived in South Korea, let alone at the location of the 38th parallel.

One has to wonder whether, if Stalin had known of America's shortfall and lack of preparedness, he would have allowed his troops, or quite possibly even ordered his troops, to cross the 38th Parallel, and just keep going. This is, of course, open to conjecture, but it is certainly an extremely interesting topic to look in to and discuss. If Soviet forces had kept going, what would have happened if troops from both sides had met further down in South Korea? Would the Russians have then retreated back to the 38th parallel, or would fighting between the two nations begin at that time? The Americans were genuinely surprised at Stalin's compliance in halting his troops at the 38th parallel.

Forces under the command of United States Lieutenant General John R. Hodge, finally arrived in Inchon on 8 September 1945 to officially accept the surrender of Imperial Japanese forces who were stationed south of the 38th Parallel.

Lieutenant General Hodge had another important role to play in relation to South Korea; he was appointed as its military governor and the man in charge of the United States Army Military Government. I have no way of knowing what he thought about the role or what lay ahead of him, but it was always going to be an interesting one because it was never going to be just about accepting the surrender of a few hundred Japanese soldiers and getting them out of there. Japan hadn't occupied Korea just since the outbreak of the war in 1939, they had been there since 1910.

It is estimated that at the time of their surrender in 1945, the Japanese civilian population living in South Korea was somewhere in the region of 700,000. It would be fair to say that the Japanese were well integrated in to every aspect of Korean life. In fact between 1938 and 1943, 802,047 Koreans applied to enlist in the Imperial Japanese Army, which suggests that life in Korea by 1945 was one more akin to a fully integrated society rather than being an occupied nation. After the war, 148 Koreans were found guilty of war crimes, twenty-three of whom were sentenced to death.

Hodge didn't get off to the best of starts in his new role; he made the decision to restore Japanese colonial administrators, who were in charge of local matters, much like a local council would in the UK, in an attempt to establish control over the civilian population. He had either totally misread the situation, or had been ill-advised. The Koreans, who at long last saw a real chance of independence, poured out in their thousands on to the streets of towns and cities throughout the American occupied southern half of the country to demonstrate. They sent out a clear and unequivocal message to the Americans that they were not prepared to return to their old way of life. Seeing such a response, Hodge quickly reversed his decision, although he still kept a number of Koreans in their previously held government positions. Remembering, of course, that these individuals had worked and collaborated with the Japanese-run colonial government, which included members of the Korean National Police Force, this was also a somewhat debateable decision.

The Japanese Emperor, Hirohito, announced his country's surrender on 15 August 1945, the relevant documentation was formally signed on 2 September, finally bringing to an end the hostilities of the Second World War.

Hirohito's announcement brought with it many issues for the Japanese, some of which were relevant to Korea because of the large Japanese civilian population that existed there, along with the properties and land that many of these people and their businesses owned. Because of the worries over the safety of the Japanese people in Korea, the now defeated Imperial Japanese authorities requested that the Koreans quickly establish a government.

The Committee for the Preparation of Korean Independence (CPKI), under the leadership of Lyuh Woon-hyung, a Korean politician whose ultimate goal was for an independent and reunified Korea, was formed. Its purpose was to set up local committees across Korea, so that the transition to independence could be coordinated.

On 28 August 1945, the CPKI announced that to ensure calm and prevent wide-scale acts of public disorder, it would act as a temporary government of Korea, and just two weeks later, on 12 September, activists of the same committee met in Seoul and announced the formation of the People's Republic of Korea.

Despite the positive and forward thinking of Lyuh Woon-hyung and his fellow members of the CPKI, who had proclaimed themselves as the temporary national government of Korea, the United States Army Military Government refused to recognise them, because of the suspected Communist sympathies held by some of its members.

As had been agreed by the Foreign Ministers of the Soviet Union, the United Kingdom, and the United States of America at the Moscow Conference of December 1945, one of the aims of the conference was for Korea to be an independent state within five years. This was not something that was totally appreciated by all elements of Korean society. This resulted in rioting in towns and cities throughout South Korea, and led to numerous cases of workers going on strike.

To countenance this threat, the Americans banned all strikes as from 8 December 1945, which simply enflamed the situation even more. But not too many people would have seen America's next move. Lieutenant Colonel Hodge took the decision to outlaw the People's Republic of Korea's

Revolutionary Government, and the People's Republic of Korea People's Committees. All this achieved was a lot more civil unrest, and eventually resulted in Hodge having no other option than to declare martial law.

Due to frustration at a collective lack of progress in the reunification process of Korea, the United States came up with the idea of holding an election, under the guidance of the United Nations. One would think that such a suggestion would be well supported, as ultimately a united Korea was the end game for both sides. Sadly, North Korea was having none of it. Neither the Soviet authorities nor the Korean Communists agreed to cooperate in such an election, stating that the idea was 'not fair', although it was never made clear why this was the case.

I believe that the real reason behind why the Soviet authorities and the Korean Communists refused to take part in the election was a concern that it would lead to a united, but non-Communist controlled, Korea. There were also a number of South Korean politicians who, because of a lack of trust in such a process, also refused to take part. It is quite feasible that their refusal was born of a fear of a Communist victory in such an election.

Elections did in fact go ahead, albeit separately: in the south, on 10 May 1948, and in the north on 25 August 1948. This resulted in a South Korean government under the leadership of Syngman Rhee, who became the inaugural President of South Korea on 20 July 1948, with the Republic of South Korea being officially established on 15 August 1948. In North Korea it was Kim Il-Sung, who became the President of the Communist controlled Democratic People's Republic of Korea, which came in to being on 9 September 1948. Soviet forces withdrew from North Korea a short while later, followed in 1949 by American forces pulling out of South Korea.

There was little or no trust between the two sides, with both countries believing the other was planning an invasion. There had been a number of clashes along the border which had resulted in thousands of deaths on both sides. Insurgencies into the South by guerrillas backed by the regime in North Korea, continued until about May 1949.

It was no secret that South Korea under Rhee had an ultimate goal of a unified democratic Korea, while the North under Kim wanted a unified socialist Korea. But how either sought to bring that about was unclear.

Whether it was simply out of a desire to invade South Korea, or to defend itself from an attack by them, Kim believed that widespread uprisings throughout the south had weakened the South Korean military and that an invasion by North Korean forces, would be welcomed by much of the South Korean population.

Initially Stalin did not think the time was right for a war in Korea. There was a civil war going on in China which ultimately saw the Communist forces of Mao Zedong's People's Liberation Army come out on top, but it had taken quite a while.

Stalin calculated that the Americans would not be interested in becoming involved in a war in Korea, which was of no real strategic importance to them. The Soviet Union authorities had also managed to crack the codes used by the United States in communications with their embassy in Moscow. Having been informed of the content of some of the messages, Stalin was convinced that Korea did not have the importance to the United States that would warrant a nuclear confrontation. Taking all this in to account, Stalin decided on a more aggressive strategy in Asia, which included the promise of economic and military aid to China.

In March 1949, Kim travelled to Moscow to attempt to persuade Joseph Stalin to give his permission to carry out an attack on the South, in what he saw as being a quick and successful war.

In April 1950, Stalin gave Kim the permission he sought to invade South Korea, but only on the condition that the Chinese leader, Mao Zedong, agreed to provide North Korea with reinforcements if needed. For Kim, the success of such an undertaking would be the fulfilment of his goal to once again reunite Korea as one nation. Stalin made it clear to Kim that he would not allow Soviet forces to openly engage in combat as part of the invasion, because he wanted to avoid a war with the United States. Kim met with Chairman Mao in May 1950. Mao was concerned that committing Chinese forces to an invasion of the South would result in the involvement of the United States in support of the South Koreans. But China desperately needed the economic and military aid that Stalin had promised. When Kim managed to secure Mao's commitment, North Korea accelerated her preparations for the invasion of the south.

North Korean forces invaded South Korea on 25 June 1950. After three years of war, fighting between the two sides ceased on 27 July 1953, with the signing of an armistice which restored the original boundary between the two countries at the 38th parallel.

Neither side had won, yet an estimated 3 million Korean people were killed or died as a result of the war, which was a higher proportional civilian death toll than had been experienced in the Second World War.

To this day (2020) Korea is still a divided nation along the 38th parallel, and as no peace treaty was ever signed and agreed, technically a state of war still remains in place between the two nations.

Chapter Eleven

British and Commonwealth Regiments in the Korean war

The Korean war saw troops from five Commonwealth countries take part. These included Australia, Canada, India, New Zealand and the United Kingdom. Collectively they were known as the British Commonwealth Forces Korea, and formed the 1st Commonwealth Division, as a rapid reaction force of the United Nations.

The troops deployed to Korea included Signals, Artillery, Engineers, Armour, Medical, Logistics, and Infantry.

Artillery
- 45th Field Regiment, Royal Artillery, July – November 1951, 25 pounder.
- 11th (Sphinx) Battery, Royal Artillery, July – November 1951, 4.2 inch mortars.
- 170th Light Battery, Royal Artillery, July – November 1951, 4.2 inch mortars.
- 14th Field Regiment, Royal Artillery, November 1951 – December 1952, 25 pounder.
- 120th Light AA Battery, Royal Artillery, October 1951 – December 1952, 4.2 inch mortars.
- 42nd Light AA Battery, Royal Artillery, November 1951 – February 1952, 4.2 inch mortars.
- 61st Light Field Regiment, January 1952 – July 1953, 4.2 inch mortars.
- 20th Field Regiment, Royal Artillery, December 1952 – July 1953, 25 pounder.
- 16th Field Regiment, Royal New Zealand Artillery, July 1951 – July 1953, 25 pounder.

- 42nd Field Regiment, Royal Artillery, December 1953 –, 25 pounder.
- 2nd Regiment, Royal Canadian Horse, July 1951 – May 1952, 25 pounder.
- 1st Regiment, Royal Canadian Horse Artillery, May 1952 – April 1953, 25 pounder.
- 81st Field Regiment, Royal Canadian Artillery, April 1953 – July 1953, 25 pounder.
- 74th (Battleax Company) Medium Battery, Royal Artillery, March – November 1953, 5.5 inch medium guns.
- 1903 Independent Air Observation Post Flight, Royal Artillery, July 1951 – July 1953.

Engineers
- 28th Field Engineer Regiment, Royal Engineers, July 1951 – July 1953.
- 64th Field Park Squadron, Royal Engineers, July 1951 – July 1953.

Armour
- 8th Kings Royal Irish Hussars, July 1951 – December 1951, Centurion tank.
- C Squadron, 7th Royal Tank Regiment, July 1951 – October 1951, Centurion tank.
- 5th Royal Inniskilling Dragoon Guards, December 1951 – December 1952, Centurion tank.
- 1st Royal Tank Regiment, December 1952 – December 1953, Centurion tank.
- 5th Royal Tank Regiment, December 1953 –, Centurion tank.
- C Squadron, Lotd Strathcona's Horse (Royal Canadian's) (2nd Armoured Regiment), May 1951 – June 1952, M4 Sherman tank.
- B Squadron, Lord Strathcona's Horse (Royal Canadians) (2nd Armoured Regiment), June 1952 – May 1953, M4 Sherman tank.
- A Squadron, Lord Strathcona's Horse (Royal Canadians) (2nd Armoured Regiment), December 1953 –, M4 Sherman tank.

Medical
- 60th (Para) Indian Field Ambulance, November 1950 – August 1953.
- 26th Field Ambulance, Royal Army Medical Corps, December 1950 –.
- No 25 Field Ambulance, Royal Canadian Army Medical Corps, May 1951 – April 1952.
- No 25 Canadian Field Dressing Station, July 1951–.
- No 37 Field Ambulance, Royal Canadian Army Medical Corps, April 1952 – May 1953.
- No 38 Field Ambulance, Royal Army Medical Corps, May 1953 –.

Logistics
Ordnance
- No 25 Canadian Infantry Brigade Group Ordnance Company, May 1951 – January 1952.
- 28th Commonwealth Infantry Brigade Ordnance Field Park.
- 24th British Infantry Brigade Group Ordnance Field Park.
- 1st Commonwealth Division, Stores Distribution Detachment.

Workshops
- 10th Infantry Workshops, Royal Electrical and Mechanical Engineers.
- 11th Infantry Workshops, Royal Electrical and Mechanical Engineers.
- 16th Infantry Workshops, Royal Electrical and Mechanical Engineers.
- 25th Canadian Support Workshop, Royal Electrical and Mechanical Engineers. May 1951 – January 1952.
- 191st Infantry Workshop, Royal Canadian Electrical and Mechanical Engineers. May 1951 – April 1955.
- 40th Canadian Infantry Workshop, Royal Canadian Electrical and Mechanical Engineers. April 1953 – December 1953.
- 42nd Infantry Workshop, Royal Canadian Electrical and Mechanical Engineers. March 1952 – February 1953.
- 1st Commonwealth Division, Tank Workshop.
- 1st Commonwealth Division, Signals Workshop.
- 1st Commonwealth Division, Recovery Unit.

Transport
- 54th Company, Royal Canadian Army Medical Corps.
- 57th Company, Royal Canadian Army Medical Corps
- 78th Company, Royal Army Service Corps
- No. 10 Company Royal New Zealand Army Service Corps. 1951–1956.

Infantry
- 25th Canadian Infantry Brigade.
- 1st Battalion, The Royal Canadian Regiment, April 1952 – March 1953.
- 2nd Battalion, The Royal Canadian Regiment, February 1951 – April 1952.
- 3rd Battalion, The Royal Canadian Regiment.
- 1st Battalion, Princess Patricia's Canadian Light Infantry. October 1951 – November 1952.
- 2nd Battalion, Princess Patricia's Canadian Light Infantry, July 1951 – November 1952.
- 3rd Battalion, Princess Patricia's Canadian Light Infantry, March 1953 – July 1953.
- 1st Battalion, Royal 22nd Regiment, April 1952 – April 1953.
- 2nd Battalion, Royal 22nd Régiment, July 1951 – April 1952.
- 3rd Battalion, Royal 22nd Régiment, April 1953 – July 1953.
- 27th Infantry Brigade (27th British Commonwealth Brigade), 1st Battalion, Middlesex Regiment.
- 1st Battalion, Argyll and Sutherland Highlanders.
- 2nd Battalion, Princess Patricia's Canadian Light Infantry, December 1950 – April 1951.
- 3rd Battalion, Royal Australian Regiment, September 1950 – April 1951.
- 16th Field Regiment, Royal New Zealand Artillery, January 1951 – April 1951.
- 60th Indian Field Ambulance.
- 28th Commonwealth Infantry Brigade (previously organised as 27th British Commonwealth Brigade).
- 1st Battalion King's Own Scottish Borderers, April 1951 – August 1952.

- 1st Battalion, King's Own Shropshire Light Infantry, July 1951 – September 1952.
- 1st Battalion, Royal Fusiliers, August 1952 – July 1953.
- 1st Battalion, Durham Light Infantry, September 1952 – July 1953.
- 3rd Battalion, Royal Australian Regiment, July 1951 – July 1953.
- 1st Battalion, Royal Australian Regiment, June 1952 – March 1953.
- 2nd Battalion, Royal Australian Regiment, April 1953 – July 1953.
- 29th Infantry Brigade, previously organised as the 29th Independent Infantry Brigade.
- 1st Battalion, Royal Northumberland Fusiliers, July 1951 – October 1951.
- 1st Battalion, Gloucestershire Regiment, July 1951 – November 1951.
- 1st Battalion, Royal Ulster Rifles, July 1951 – October 1951.
- 1st Battalion, Royal Norfolk Regiment, October 1951 – September 1952.
- 1st Battalion, Leicestershire Regiment, October 1951 – June 1952.
- 1st Battalion, Welch Regiment, November 1951 – November 1952.
- 1st Battalion, Black Watch, June 1952 – July 1953.
- 1st Battalion, King's Regiment (Liverpool), September 1952 – July 1953.
- 1st Battalion, Duke of Wellington's Regiment, September 1952 – July 1953.
- 1st Battalion, Royal Scots, July 1953.

From all of these fine regiments, almost 100,000 British soldiers saw service in the Korean war, some of them were veterans of the Second World War, while others were new recruits, having been too young to have served prior to this.

It is a war that has been described as 'The Forgotten War', because it came along before there was a TV set in every living room across the nation, and the British public, who were still experiencing rationing after the end of the Second World War, had no real appetite for yet another war.

A number of those who served did so as part of their National Service and once they had served their mandatory two years in the armed services (increased from 18 months with the outbreak of the Korean war), they simply returned to their pre-war jobs and lives. National Service began in 1949 and finally ended with the last of the National Service men being demobbed in May 1963. National Service required men aged between 17 and 21 years of age to undertake either military service or some form of war related work. Initially this was for a period of eighteen months, after which time they would remain on the reserve list for a further four years. Because of Britain's involvement in the Korean War, the period of National Service was increased to two years.

It was also described as 'Britain's own Vietnam', a reference to the Vietnam War which, in different guises, raged between 1 November 1955 and 30 April 1975, and saw America lose 58,318 of its young men, of which one in five were non-combat related, which equates to 11,664 died while serving in Vietnam, but not in, or as a result of, combat. A further 303,644 US service men were wounded during the war.

With the Korean war coming to an end on 25 June 1953, and the Vietnam War commencing on 1 November 1955, there would have been many American servicemen who would have fought in both wars, and others who would have also fought in the Second World War.

In Closing

Having researched this book it quickly became apparent to me that writing it would also have to include looking at the background, history and timeline of how the Korean war came about. I felt that this was an important aspect of the book, because it was, after all, the war which resulted in the acts of bravery that saw, Lieutenant Colonel James Power Carne, DSO, Major Kenneth Muir, Lieutenant Philip Kenneth Edward Curtis, and Private William Speakman, all awarded the Victoria Cross, and Lieutenant Terence Edward Waters and Fusilier Derek Godfrey Kinne, awarded the George Medal.

Putting aside the acts of supreme bravery and gallantry that this book is ultimately about, I have come to the conclusion that the war was both unnecessary and a complete waste of time. In reality, there was absolutely no need for it to have ever taken place. When the Second World War came to end after Japan's surrender, Korea could have been left to sort their own internal politics. When France was liberated from Nazi occupation, she wasn't split in two and placed under the control of foreign powers; instead, the differing political factions were left to retake control of their country and sort out whatever internal problems they had.

Once Japan had surrendered and her troops had been rounded up and taken as prisoners of war, why was there any further need for foreign troops to remain in the country? What right did the Soviet Union, America or China have to determine how another country should be run politically? Surely it was for the people and politicians of Korea to determine their own destiny, no matter what that turned out to be.

The war ended up involving twenty different countries, which included both South and North Korea. On the United Nations' side, their casualties included 170,927 dead and missing with 566,493 wounded. As for North

Korea, it is estimated she lost an estimated 500,000 men who were killed, along with a further 208,729 from China. There were a total of 686,500 North Korean and Chinese wounded. For a war that did not have to be, it was a staggering waste of life.

Having said all of that, the bravery and valour of the men who took part in the war is not open to question.

Appendix

The viewpoint of a modern soldier in combat

I spoke to my younger son who served with 2 and 3 Para during two tours of Afghanistan during 2009 and 2010. The question I asked him was, 'what is it like just before you go out on patrol and when you come into a contact situation with the enemy?' I checked with him first to make sure he was OK speaking about such matters, as he had been injured while serving there on his first tour, and had lost a number of comrades on that same tour. The last thing I wanted to do was to raise demons in him that he had long ago dealt with and laid to rest. He was willing to talk to me on the subject.

> First off Dad, you have to remember I was only 19 years of age at the time, a young man still in my teens, who other than a day trip to France, was not well travelled. If I am being totally honest with myself, I would also accept that I was still somewhat immature.
>
> Basic training as you will remember was tough, and out of the 108 of us who began to course, there were only twelve of us left by the time it came to the pass out parade, which I might add was a massive moral and confidence booster for me. I had proved to myself, you, Mum and my friends that I had what it took to achieve something, which was important to me, and certainly made me feel good about myself.

It was good hearing him speak about this stage of his life in such positive terms, because my recollection is that the weekly drop-out rate on his course was absolutely staggering. Many of those who fell by the wayside were individuals who my son considered to be high achievers and better than he was on the course, so every time one of them dropped out, his confidence went through the roof.

Afghanistan was slightly different to most wars of the twentieth century, in so far as many of the deaths and injuries were caused by IEDs, Improvised Explosive Devices, or mines. For most soldiers, myself included, the worry about being out on a foot patrol, was being killed or maimed by such devices. It was a worry that was constantly on your mind, and meant you spent most of your time staring intently down on the ground, and following in the footsteps of the man in front of you, rather than scanning ahead and taking in your surroundings, looking for and noticing potential enemy combatants.

I eagerly awaited his description of what it felt like being involved in a contact with enemy combatants.

I will give you a first-hand account of what a contact felt like. Firstly, time seems to stand still. It's like everything goes in to slow motion. There was this time I was on a patrol with my colleagues when we came under attack from the Taliban. We had just entered a village and were strung out in single file, it was relatively quiet, but there were a few people hanging around. Then all of a sudden and without any warning, everybody did a star burst and disappeared. I knew straight away what was about to happen. No sooner had they got out of sight, than all hell broke loose. They opened up on us from all directions. Initially I froze, only for a split second in reality, but at the time it felt like a lifetime. The guy in front of me took a round in his lower leg. I can still see it now, just hanging on by a thread as he fell to the ground. I remember a couple of rounds go pinging past my head, I heard that distinctive sound a bullet makes when it goes past you so close, that it is as close as it can possibly be without actually hitting you. I honestly thought the next one was going to have my name on it, but thankfully it didn't. Then all of a sudden my training kicked in and I made for cover and returned fire, although I didn't actually know who or what I was firing at. As quick as the fire fight had begun, it was over, and the Taliban fighters slipped away in the confusion and had long gone before we had got our act together.

'And how did you feel while all of this was going on?' I asked.

Initially it was fear, fear that I was going to be killed. My heart was beating so fast it sounded like a helicopter in the middle of my chest. I could almost hear the noise of it in my head. My mouth was dry, my hands were sweaty, and I wanted to look up to see where the Taliban were, but every time the sound of gunfire rained down on us, we just wanted to ensure we were in cover. Having said all of that, it wasn't till afterwards and we had made it back to our base, that I really had the opportunity to fully comprehend what I had been through and managed to survive. Having said all of that, it didn't get any easier the next time we went out on patrol.

About the Author

Stephen is a happily retired police officer having served with Essex Police as a constable for thirty years between 1983 and 2013. He is married to Tanya who is also his best friend.

Both Stephen's sons, Luke and Ross, were members of the armed forces, collectively serving five tours of Afghanistan between 2008 and 2013. Both were injured on their first tour. This led to his first book: *Two Sons in a Warzone – Afghanistan: The True Story of a Father's Conflict*, which was published in October 2010.

Both of Stephen's grandfathers served in and survived the First World War, one with the Royal Irish Rifles, the other in the Mercantile Navy; while his father was a member of the Royal Army Ordnance Corp during and after the Second World War.

Stephen corroborated with one of his writing partners, Ken Porter, on a previous book published in August 2012, *German POW Camp 266 – Langdon Hills*. It spent six weeks as the number one bestselling book in Waterstones, Basildon, between March and April 2013. They have also collaborated on four books in the Towns & Cities in the Great War series by Pen and Sword. Stephen has also written other titles for the same series of books, and in February 2017 his book, *The Surrender of Singapore – Three Years of Hell 1942–45*, was published. This was followed in March 2018 by *Against All Odds: Walter Tull the Black Lieutenant*. October 2018 saw the publication of *Animals in the Great War*; in January 2019, *A History of the Royal Hospital Chelsea – 1682–2017 – The Warriors Repose*. These last two books were written with his wife, Tanya. March 2019 saw the publication of *Disaster before D-Day: Unravelling the Tragedy of Slapton Sands*. In March 2020, *Mystery of Missing Flight F-BELV*, the personal story of the death of Stephen's uncle during the Vietnam war. The same month saw the publication of *City of London at War 1939–45*. April 2020 saw the publication of *Holocaust: The Nazis' Wartime Jewish Atrocities*. In June 2020, *Churchill's Flawed Decisions: Errors in Office of the Greatest Briton*, was published.

Stephen has co-written three crime thrillers which were published between 2010 and 2012, and centre round a fictional detective named Terry Danvers.

When he is not writing, Stephen and Tanya enjoy the simplicity of going out for a morning coffee, or walking their four German Shepherd dogs early each morning while most sensible people are still fast asleep in their beds.

Index

Aden Emergency, 16

Allnut, Private Roland, 84–5

Argyll and Sutherland
  Highlanders, 23, 26, 36–7,
  44–51, 53–5, 57–8, 69

Bissett, VC, Major W.D., 58

Black Watch (Royal Highland
  Regiment), 17–18, 23–4

British & Commonwealth
  Regiments in Korea, 104–108

Buchanan, Captain Neil, 37

Cairo Conference, 95–6

Campbell, VC, Brigadier
  Lorne M., 58

Carne, VC DSO, Lieutenant-Colonel
  James Power, 9, 32–4, 37–43

Chinese People's Volunteer Army,
  66, 69

Courtney, Company Sergeant
  Major Arthur, 91

Curtis, VC, Lieutenant Philip
  Kenneth Edward, 27–9, 31–3, 110

Davey, Leading Seaman Brian, 46

Duke of Cornwall's Light Infantry,
  27, 31, 33

Edwards, Captain, 17

English, David John, 68

Fairhurst, Lance Corporal, 56

Gloucestershire Regiment, 29, 31,
  33–4, 36–8, 39, 41, 43, 60, 63,
  66–9, 82–4, 86, 90–1

Graham, VC, Colonel
  Sir Reginald, 58

Hill, Private, 56

Hirohito, Emperor, 99–100

Horsfall, Private Ronald, 67

Hutchison, Colonel J.R.H., 89

Il-Sung, Kim, 1, 3, 6, 79, 81, 101

Imjin River, Battle of, 29, 31, 33,
  39, 41, 61, , 67, 70–1, 74, 82, 91

Jones, Private Leonard Allison, 67

Kings Own Scottish Borderers, 11,
  14–15, 17–18, 20, 23–4, 26, 107

Kinne, GC, Fusilier Derek
  Godfrey, vii, 69–74, 77, 110

Korean People's Army, 1–2, 13,
  38, 48

Leicestershire Regiment, 36, 108
London Gazette, 19, 23, 32, 34,
    40–2, 51, 61, 71

MacArthur, General Douglas,
    1, 57, 79–80, 97
MacIntyre, VC, Captain D.L., 59
Malayan Communist Party, 15
Malayan National Liberation
    Army, 15
Middlesex Regiment, 36–7, 46–7, 57
Military Police, 16
Mortlock, Private John, 86
Muir, VC, Major Kenneth, 9, 23,
    44–56, 59, 110
Murdoch, Sergeant-Major Busty, 22

O'Sullivan, Sergeant, 57
Other military crisis, 93–4

Pigg, Sergeant, 55–6
Potsdam Conference, 96
Purves, DSO, 2nd Lieutenant
    William, 26

Radfan Campaign, 16
Renouf, Private Joe, 86
Rhee, President Syngman, 1, 3,
    101–102

Royal Army Medical Corps, 19
Royal Hospital Chelsea, 9, 22, 24
Royal Northumberland Fusiliers,
    36, 60, 69, 71, 74–5, 83
Royal Ulster Rifles, 36, 69, 83, 91

Speakman, VC, Private Bill,
    9–26, 110
Special Air Service, 15–16
Stonehouse, Private William, 86
Streeter, Private Reginald, 37, 57

Taylor, Private Tam, 37, 58
Truman, President Harry S., 8, 61,
    79–80, 89, 92, 96–7

United Nations Memorial
    Cemetery, Busan, 24, 31,
    66, 76–7

Warburton, Sapper John, 17
Ward, Lance Corporal, 56–7
Waters, GC, Lieutenant Terence
    Edward, 60–3, 66–7, 110
Watkin Williams, Major John, 91
Watts, Private, 56–7
Whittick, Paul, 19
Williams, Private Cecil Roy, 68
Woon-hyung, Lyuh, 100